To: Brian Smith
Here's to a world that
is filled with fully
respectful, peak
performance leaders!

Your friend,
Janet Meeks

Gracious
Leadership

Lead Like You've Never
Led Before

Janet Smith Meeks

Smart Business Books
An Imprint of Smart Business Network, Inc.

Published by:
Smart Business Network
835 Sharon Drive, Suite 200
Westlake, OH 44145

Printed in the United States of America
Editor: Dustin S. Klein

ISBN: 978-1-945389-86-3
Library of Congress Control Number: 2017958344

*In Memory
of My Parents*

*James Edwin Smith, Sr.
Marcelene Cobb Smith*

Advance Praise for Gracious Leadership

"Janet Meeks tells a personal, clearly articulated story of learning and practicing 'Gracious Leadership' and its central importance to mission success. Hers is a timeless, head and heart journey that reveals a path for all of us."

— *C. Robert Kidder, director, Merck & Co.; former board chairman, Chrysler; former lead director, Morgan Stanley; former CEO, Duracell; former CEO, Borden Inc.*

"*Gracious Leadership*, by Janet Smith Meeks, shares the powerful, personal examples of how passionate, brave, courageous and communicative leaders deliver tremendous value to all their constituencies and are truly the recipe for organizational and personal success!"

— *Kerrii B. Anderson, former president & CEO, Wendy's International; corporate director, Worthington Industries and Labcorp; chairman, Elon University*

"Continuous learning is not always about learning something new, but reminding yourself of the important things you may have forgotten. Seasoned leaders who read *Gracious Leadership* and utilize the Conversation Starters will help refresh and refine their own leadership competencies and create a great learning experience for their teams.

When I talk with folks about what I have learned over the years, I always tell them they should handle disappointments with grace as it will be remembered and pay dividends in the future. Janet's book reminds me there are many other opportunities where grace can be applied to everyone's advantage.

Janet's comments that great leaders recognize they don't have all the answers are spot on. They are not afraid to ask the people who do have the answers the right questions, no matter what level these folks may be. And when they ask, gracious leaders listen like no one else is in the room."

— *Mike Kaufmann, CEO, Cardinal Health, a Fortune 100 company*

"Gracious Leadership is more than a book, it is a case study of one individual—the author, who describes her experiences from childhood and family values to the impact family values had on a career in both the financial and health care industries. A successful and remarkable CEO, the author emphasizes that the basic principles of Gracious Leadership are transferrable regardless of corporate, organizational or even government focus. Perhaps, and most importantly, the author provides insights as to why some leaders miss the mark.

Janet Meeks has blessed us with a documentary, a guideline, a new label and introduction of a completely new description of the attributes of Gracious Leadership. Regardless of position, title or responsibility, or even type of organization, I find this work to be more than insightful.

Early in my reading, I knew I had to complete this work when I noted the following words from the author: 'I believe teams of all types within all industries and organizations can reap great rewards from displaying gracious and respectful behaviors as they seek to optimize their collective performance. This holds true at home, on the basketball court, in the C-suite, or in the Boardroom.' The preceding words clearly established that Gracious Leadership is about a focus on people, the people within the organization who ultimately make the organization what it is or becomes.

I wish I had this work many years ago. Janet Meeks has given us a glimpse at her life journey and the 13 attributes of Gracious Leadership in a learning and teachable format. This work goes beyond the definitions and principles of leadership described in Jim Collins' legendary work *Good to Great* first released in 2001. This work is a must read for all who really believe that we, as individuals and organizations, succeed via the quality and excellence in how we serve and recognize others for the contributions they make!"

— *John Fleming, Author, Consultant and Speaker; former Publisher/Editor-In-Chief of Direct Selling News; former senior executive of Avon Products, Inc.*

"*Gracious Leadership: Lead Like You've Never Led Before* provides invaluable insights into leadership—real and true leadership. The Key

Ingredients shared by Janet are precisely those required for GREAT leadership. Whether you are just beginning your journey to become a world class leader or you have many years in your role as a leader, Janet's insights are inspiring and remind us all what is important in developing ourselves to our fullest potential.

I have been blessed to know Janet for many years. She is impressive beyond words, brilliant, compassionate and someone who truly cares for others. Janet's spirit and affirmation of her undying FAITH are both humble and bold. She continues to be an amazing role model to many. I am honored to be one of many people who has benefitted from her wisdom. Enjoy *Gracious Leadership*. A world full of gracious leaders—Janet's aspiration—would make our organizations and communities a wonderful place. Let's all lead like we never have led before—starting today."

— *Dwight Smith, Servant Leader, chairman & CEO, Sophisticated Systems, Inc.; founder,*
My Special Word

"In corporate America's drive for growth and profit, many organizations have created a workforce of the 'walking wounded.' Employees within these companies leave their souls at the front door and steel themselves against daily insults, indifference and condescending behavior from executives and managers entrusted to lead them. There simply is a better way. Employees thirst for compassionate leadership that honors rather than strips them of their dignity—the kind of leadership that Janet Meeks masterfully details in *Gracious Leadership*. In this book, Janet shares leadership strategies that can deliver exceptional results by transforming companies with toxic cultures into high performing organizations driven by engaged employees who are walking tall!"

— *Barbara J. Smoot, CEO, WELD (Women for Economic and Leadership Development);*
commissioner, Columbus Women's Commission; corporate director, National Church
Residences; former vice president, Nationwide Financial

"Readers may be easily overwhelmed by the hundreds of leadership books with catchy titles lining the shelves of bookstores these days. With the publication of *Gracious Leadership: Lead Like You've*

Never Led Before, Janet Meeks has made a unique contribution to the collection. Her description of the key ingredients of Gracious Leadership draws not only from the research literature but from the personal stories (hers and others) of successful leaders. Her treatment is 'elegant in its simplicity.' Although it may seem simplistic to say that effective leaders demonstrate both 'head and heart' competencies, Janet provides the reader with true stories of how this dynamic duo looks in action!

Gracious Leadership is an easy read of complex issues. One cannot help but become personally engaged in each short, crisp chapter. I recommend that this book be required reading for graduate students in healthcare administration, MBA students focusing on healthcare, mid-career healthcare professionals who are transitioning into leadership roles from clinical and/or business roles, and those 'high potentials' who have been identified in their organizations as having growth opportunities in their organizations. Upon reflection, I think that leaders at every career stage will take a step forward by not only reading the book but applying the Conversation Starters that the author includes after each chapter."

— *Peter J. Giammalvo, PhD, leadership & talent management consultant; retired healthcare executive-in-residence & visiting professor, College of Health Sciences & Professions, Ohio University; former Chief Learning Officer, Vanderbilt University Medical Center*

"Gracious Leadership provides golden opportunities for any leader to be set apart in today's competitive landscape. Through applying these important leadership lessons such as walking in the shoes of those who follow you and matching passion with purpose, you can lead your team to deliver peak performance results for your business and your customers."

— *Cindy Monroe, founder & CEO, Thirty-One Gifts*

Table of Contents

Foreword

When Janet asked me to write the introduction for this book, I was humbled and nervous. Paraphrasing the immortal words of Wayne and Garth from Wayne's World, "I'm not worthy! I'm not worthy!" How could I contribute to this magnificent book in a truly meaningful way?

First, I was very intrigued by the title selected for the book, Gracious Leadership. As I thought about it, I immediately did what I often do when a word causes me to think deeply—I looked up the definition of "gracious" and found the following descriptions: courtesy, kind, pleasant; generosity of spirit; kindness and warm courtesy; compassionate; and showing divine grace. There is indeed something divine about a great leader; each of us recognizes the magical "presence" of gracious leaders and how special they are when we have been blessed to experience them.

This book is an outstanding compendium of leadership revelations that Janet has synthesized over her career. I think that the term "gracious" is not only a reflection of Janet's insights from her leadership journey, but it also describes my experience with Janet as a leader. In the words of Jim Collins' *Good to Great* themes, Janet is indeed a "Level 5" leader, and it is the reason why it was an easy decision for me to support the decision for her to lead a hospital before having operations experience. I believe that her life transformation, coupled with great mentors and an untraditional career path, have made her a gracious leader who is generously sharing her learnings with us in this book.

I resonate with every concept and insight in this book, especially the "head-heart" connection that Janet discusses in the third chapter. In my early career as a leader, I prided myself on my technical knowledge, but I realized very quickly that leadership is about how we engage with others in a caring and meaningful way. Teddy Roosevelt was quoted as saying "People don't care how much you know until they know how much you care!" Gracious leaders understand it is all about cultivating relationships and caring for others. They know their power comes from others, and influence trumps control. They know devoting time for dialogue on the "why and how" is as important as the "what." And gracious leaders know lasting change requires consideration of the four dimensions of people, process, technology, and culture.

Janet recognizes that leadership isn't about "soft stuff." Graceful leaders know that tough love is also important; other critical and compassionate aspects of leadership are developing clear goals and measures and holding people accountable for performance. If a leader is transparent, caring, and engaged, then the leader must expect the same from his or her people if the organization's mission is to be accomplished.

The book covers 13 important attributes of gracious leaders and contains suggestions on how to make Gracious Leadership real. I especially appreciate the fact that each chapter describes an attribute in a clear and practical way, combined with real life experiences. Finally, there are powerful questions for leaders to consider. The book is formatted in an ideal way to use as part of a "journal club" discussion for leaders who wish to learn together through deep discussion of a chapter and the "conversation starter" questions.

In my own life, I have learned from many gracious leaders who had confidence in me and gave me challenging assignments that were well outside of my comfort zone. I made many mistakes and learned from those mistakes with the help of these mentors. They shaped who I am as a person. They have moved me away from "downward spiral thinking" and have helped me see the possibilities. I have done my best to give back by supporting the growth and development of those I serve—so they can follow after I'm gone by leading and serving with soul. While I don't always live by my own words, my motto has been that the most important things in life are faith in God, love of family and friends, good health, happiness, and the ability to serve others.

It is my hope that this book inspires you to think about those who have mentored you and how you can use the meaningful attributes of Gracious Leadership that Janet has outlined to continue to refine and shape your effectiveness to serve others.

Peace to you,

Mike Slubowski
President and Chief Operating Officer, Trinity Health

Prologue

I was raised in the heart of the South within a multi-generational family of native Mississippians. At the time of my father's birth, his parents had moved briefly to Cotton Valley, Louisiana. Economic times were tough, and Papa Smith had to leave Mississippi temporarily to find work in the oilfields of the Bayou State.

My loving parents believed that "Please" and "Thank you" were non-negotiable expressions of basic respect. As a child, little did I know that such seemingly small requirements would serve as the foundation for many of my future leadership convictions.

I believe teams of all types, within all industries and organizations, can reap great rewards from displaying gracious and respectful behaviors as they seek to optimize their collective performance. This holds true at home, on the basketball court, in the C-Suite, or in the Boardroom.

As we explore the topic of Gracious Leadership, I will share with you some of the memories from my own leadership journey.

I trust these stories will bring to life some of the opportunities you may encounter as you seek to refine your personal effectiveness as a leader. My hope is you will be challenged to leverage those leadership attributes that represent your strengths and to improve within those areas where you can become a better leader.

To facilitate this process, I have included at the end of applicable chapters a series of Conversation Starters. As you consider the principles of Gracious Leadership, may you be inspired to "bring to life" these philosophies as part of your own leadership beliefs.

I also encourage you to discuss the Conversation Starters with colleagues whom you will lead both now and in the future. In so doing, your team can make the most of its journey towards achieving peak performance through ultimate respect.

The lessons within this book have been gleaned from those whom I have had the honor of following or leading in some capacity. Some of these individuals have been important mentors in my professional journey. Others placed their trust in me as their leader. All of these individuals have made an equivalent impact on my life as they have helped me learn what effective, Gracious Leadership means at its very core.

Whether these individuals were my leaders or my followers, I suspect they do not fully comprehend the profound impact they have had in shaping and molding me into the leader I have become.

More importantly, the lessons I learned from them continue to inspire me every single day of my life.

It is to my family and to these individuals that *Gracious Leadership: Lead Like You've Never Led Before* is dedicated.

My dream is that these lessons of leadership will be paid forward to future generations and the positive ripple effect of Gracious Leadership will spread far and wide for many years to come.

Why?

Because Gracious Leadership is not solely about being a respectful leader in the workplace. Gracious Leadership is about being respectful to others in every aspect of our lives.

PART ONE

MY STORY

*Seemingly small acts of kindness
make a permanent imprint on
people's lives.*

Chapter One

A Transformed Life

After graduating from Carthage High School in 1973, I followed in the footsteps of my father and my brother by attending the University of Mississippi for my higher education. Immediately after graduate school at Ole Miss, I got married, moved to Tupelo, Mississippi, and started my career in the financial services industry.

My first professional mentor was Aubrey Patterson, former Chairman of the Board and Chief Executive Officer of BancorpSouth (then Bank of Mississippi). He is an awesome leader, and I learned so much from him. You will hear about Mr. Patterson in greater detail throughout this book.

All was well at work and in life. I enjoyed great friendships. I loved my church home, as well as my community. I was also expecting my first baby and had decorated the nursery to perfection in anticipation of this precious little one's arrival.

From a professional perspective, I truly enjoyed my work. I felt at home at Bank of Mississippi, and I was pleased to be experiencing rapid growth in responsibility. In fact, I was confident I would be a career banker.

Yes, all was well!

An Unexpected Detour
During my fourth year of service with Bank of Mississippi, I was shocked to learn that all was not well after all. I was blindsided by a life-altering experience.

My first baby was born, and the baby died on the same day because of a fatal birth defect.

What we had expected to be a mountaintop experience had radically changed course without warning. Immediately, I found myself plunged into the deepest valley of my life. This devastating experience shook me to my core. I desperately tried to make sense out of a situation that made no sense to me at all.

You can only imagine the many unanswerable questions that I pondered.

Why had this happened to my baby when I had done everything right with regard to prenatal care?

How could this have occurred, as there was no family history of such conditions?

How could this nightmare be real when I was fully prepared to be a devoted and loving mother?

In the midst of my deepest despair, the promise that provided some semblance of hope was found in Romans 8:28, a scripture that says, "All things work together for good for those who love the Lord."

At the time, these words were easy to articulate but difficult to embrace. I struggled to understand how anything good could possibly come from this horrific experience.

Why did my baby have to die?

My faith, my family, and my friends served as the source of my strength during this turbulent time. I was grateful to be surrounded with love and support from those who were near and dear to me.

Seemingly Small Acts of Kindness

For several weeks after the baby's death, I found myself reliving this tragic loss over and over as I thought about all that had transpired.

It occurred to me while I was in the hospital that I was surrounded by healthcare professionals who, other than my doctor, did not know me. Yet these newcomers treated me like I was a member of their own families.

I thought constantly about these employees. During my hospitalization, I was in such a state of shock I could not recall their names. They did not know me from the next patient, but they shared with me their love and grace as they cared both "for" and "about" me at my point of greatest need. Their seemingly small acts of kindness made a permanent imprint on my life as they essentially helped to carry me through the deepest valley I had ever experienced.

Serendipity, Coincidence, or Calling?

During the months that followed, I developed what can only be described as an unquenchable thirst to be a part of healthcare. I wanted to find a way to help others—just as those employees supported me during my point of deepest despair.

One to two years before my baby's death, Mr. Patterson had nominated me to participate in a state-wide leadership development program called Leadership Mississippi. During this year-long curriculum, participants were divided into teams by Congressional Districts and assigned projects to pursue.

As we worked on our project over the course of several months, one of my team members, an executive from North Mississippi Medical Center, tried to recruit me. He thought I'd be a good fit with his team. While I was flattered by his kind comments, I gracefully declined his pursuit because I was happy at Bank of Mississippi.

Times, however, change. Approximately four weeks after my baby's death, I learned this same executive had announced he was moving to New York State to accept a promotion. This news reminded me about his recruitment attempt. And because I now had an insatiable desire to be a part of healthcare, I called and congratulated the executive on his exciting news.

I then asked if he thought I should apply for the job he was leaving.

He said, "Yes!"

I immediately submitted my application for the role (along with several dozen other applicants).

Four months after the death of my baby, I was offered an opportunity to become this executive's successor and join the senior leadership team of North Mississippi Medical Center (NMMC) as their Director of Public Relations and Development.

You might ask, "Why would a large medical center employ a young executive with no prior healthcare experience?"

My honest answer is, "I don't know" ... other than to believe the CEO saw potential in me, that he was aware of my professional progression as an understudy to Aubrey Patterson, that he knew I was a person of integrity, and that he was confident I could learn the business of healthcare.

Proceed with Caution

While I was personally thrilled about receiving this offer, my father cautioned me to avoid making such a move too quickly. He grew up in an era when many people went to work for one company and remained in that organization for life.

Because I had only worked at Bank of Mississippi for just under five years, my dad wanted to make sure I was being conservative, mature, and grounded in analyzing this new professional opportunity.

In addition to my father's caution, some of my colleagues counseled me to be acutely aware of the huge professional and financial risks I would be taking. Mr. Patterson strongly encouraged me to stay at the bank. Even the bank's Chairman of the Board and CEO met with me and shared his belief that I was making a huge mistake by leaving his organization.

Was I indeed about to make a mistake I would regret for years?

It was certainly true I didn't know anything about healthcare administration. Other than my short tour of duty as interim vice president of marketing at Bank of Mississippi, I had no previous training in public relations disciplines. And I had zero experience in development.

By entering the foreign territory of an "unknown to me" industry, from a professional perspective, I would clearly be starting over.

To further complicate the analysis, I had a bright future at Bank of Mississippi, with a fabulous mentor whom I revered. I had also developed very close friendships with several of my banking colleagues.

In considering only the facts, I had to agree I would definitely be taking professional and financial risks by entering an industry I understood solely from my one, very personal, very traumatic, patient experience.

Yet, even in the midst of the significant doubt and the risk associated with leaving a secure and supportive environment, my heart took over, and the rest was history. For me, there would be no turning back. I had to make the move into healthcare.

Through my experience of profound loss and the simultaneous receipt of seemingly small acts of kindness from complete strangers, I was convinced I was being "called" to serve in the healing profession of healthcare.

And although I didn't realize it at the time, taking these risks and making this professional detour would eventually become one of the most important and gratifying decisions of my life.

Notes

Be confident, humble, and secure in relying upon those who will follow you.

Chapter 2

Entering Foreign Territory

I followed my convictions and accepted the offer to work for North Mississippi Medical Center in Tupelo, at the time the largest non-metropolitan hospital in the nation.

In beginning this new professional journey, I quickly learned not to be too proud to ask others for guidance. As a newcomer, I was like a sponge, soaking up all the knowledge I could about the inner workings of a large medical center.

I asked exhaustive questions during every orientation meeting with department heads, vice presidents, and other executives with whom I would be working. I sincerely inquired as to what their jobs entailed, what they expected their employees to accomplish, and how each of their departments supported the overall success of the medical center.

I sought their feedback on the strengths and opportunities they saw within my newly inherited department and its staff. Of utmost importance, I asked them to share with me candidly what they needed from me as a peer and what they expected as future deliverables from my department.

A City Within a City

Medical centers are extraordinarily complex places. In fact, a hospital is a lot like a city within a city. For example, medical centers have restaurants, a hotel, doctors' offices, a post office, police department (security), educational facilities, libraries, and places of worship (chapels) ... not to mention the abundant clinical areas filled with complex and ever-changing technology.

Needless to say, it took several months to gain a high-level understanding of not only the general operations of the organization, but also of the massive physical plant of this very large, tertiary medical center.

I shall never forget on an early tour of the facility how I noticed directional signs that included complex clinical terminology. To a healthcare newcomer, these words seemed to be written in a foreign language ... as an example ... electroencephalography. I wondered, "What in the world is that word?" Remember, this was *before* Google, Siri, and Alexa!

Then I humbly asked someone to explain it to me.

And supportive colleagues did provide explanations to me again and again, always showing respect and consistently taking care to avoid making me feel like I was back in elementary school. For that kind assistance, I was extraordinarily grateful!

As a lifelong learner, this journey into healthcare taught me to be 100 percent comfortable in asking others for help. It also affirmed the reality I would never have all the answers on my own. As a leader, I learned I would need to be confident, humble, and secure in relying upon those who would follow me because they would clearly be the true experts within their respective areas of responsibility.

The "ABCs" of Different Businesses

So here I was, suddenly on the fast track to learn the ABCs of this new foreign territory. Every industry seems to have its own version of alphabet soup, and healthcare was no exception. To illustrate the point, banks have DDAs, MMAs, and IRAs, while hospitals have HMOs, PPOs, and ACOs. What I found surprising, however, was that similarities actually existed between the financial services industry and healthcare.

Both are complex businesses.

Banking and healthcare are relationship-based. They rely upon front line staff to build and to maintain relationships of trust that are required to create customer loyalty.

Banking and healthcare are heavily regulated by the government.

Both industries deliver an intangible product.

And banks and hospitals both must deliver extraordinary customer service.

The experience of entering my new foreign territory and seeing the similarities between it and my former profession provided an important, big picture epiphany.

From the perspective of leadership, I've realized businesses across different industrial sectors have much more in common than we might possibly imagine. I have personally found this revelation to be true throughout my career as I have served on boards and as an advisor to CEOs whose organizations transcend multiple businesses and industries.

Wide variation clearly exists in the unique ABCs of different businesses. And while the products provided across multiple sectors are vastly diverse, the strategic imperative for leaders *to deliver optimal outcomes* remains the same across all such "foreign lands."

All leaders are expected to have their teams perform with excellence across the balanced scorecard. All leaders are held accountable to provide value to customers and shareholders (as applicable). All leaders should demonstrate consistent respect to employees, partners, and other key stakeholders. And all leaders have the opportunity to achieve these expected results through applying timeless principles of effective leadership. These C-Suite deliverables are equally as applicable across all businesses, *without* regard to any foreign language or territorial boundary.

With these new revelations in mind, after one year of my journey into the new land and language of healthcare, I came to the welcomed conclusion that healthcare wasn't such a foreign territory after all!

Notes

*Show your team why you are
in business and what impact
you aspire to have on
your customers.*

Chapter Three

The Head-Heart Connection

During my early years in healthcare, our CEO brought in a leadership development consultant to support our senior team as we were collectively refining our executive skills.

As part of the pre-work for this consulting engagement, we individually had to answer survey questions about our leadership philosophies. Of all the questions posed, the most difficult question to answer was the following:

"Do you lead with (A) your head or (B) your heart?"

I wanted to check Option (C) for both.

Much to my dismay, there was no Option (C).

I begrudgingly answered that I led with my head, which seemed like the only logical answer from a business perspective.

While I do not specifically recall any definitive conversation within our leadership team about the dilemma presented through the above question, I personally thought about it a lot. Down deep inside, I knew the right answer for me as a leader would be to lead with *both* my head *and* my heart.

Perhaps this self-reflection was connected in some manner to how I had made the decision to transition from banking into healthcare. If I had based my decision solely upon the head facts that were extraordinarily compelling, I would not have left the bank. But because I had allowed my heart to have a seat at the table and interject the importance of my newfound calling, I made a decision that placed me exactly where I was intended to serve.

It was right then that I had a lightbulb moment about what I call the Head-Heart Connection.

What is the Head-Heart Connection?

Through the Head-Heart Connection, leaders should be able to make the best possible decisions in the workplace and in other aspects of their lives.

In organizations that aspire to be financially sustainable, leaders should be cautious in making heart-only decisions in isolation and without regard to the story that is told by the data, the analytics, and other relevant facts. A frequent conversation within nonprofit circles is that, "Where there is no money, there is no mission." This means that nonprofits must also be financially sound to perpetuate the mission to serve the greater good of the community.

Conversely, although you can choose to make head-based decisions solely through the application of the facts, the best decisions also consider the heart part, i.e., the broader impact upon key stakeholders.

This belief is not intended to convey that tough decisions will never have an adverse impact upon others, but rather to approach the decisions in an *enlightened* manner and minimize any negative impact or unintended consequences ... to do what is right, fair, and just.

Leading with both your head and your heart does not mean you're soft or fail to hold your team accountable to achieve the right results. Much to the contrary, when you lead with your head and your heart, you consistently act in the best interest of your key stakeholders and are purposeful in helping employees understand they are doing meaningful work.

Employees need to know they can always trust their employers to do the right thing. And employees need to experience a connection between what they are *motivated* to do through their job descriptions and what they are *inspired* to do from within their hearts.

Employees on the front line particularly need a clear line of sight between the work that they accomplish in their daily roles and the overall mission and goals of the organization. It is sad that many people go to work every day and simply go through the motions of *just doing their jobs.*

It is through the Head-Heart Connection that employees derive true fulfillment from their work. The Head-Heart Connection leads employees to develop pride in what they do every day, become loyal to their employers, and feel passionate about serving the organization's customers in an extraordinary manner.

Finding the Head-Heart Connection in Any Industry

The Head-Heart Connection can be found within any industry. You just must be intentional in looking for it.

I recently attended a presentation during which the CEO of a large, publicly-traded financial services corporation talked about the importance of helping his employees understand the higher purpose of their work. He said his employees "help to make life better for their customers."

To provide a hypothetical example, imagine that a mortgage loan officer is accountable for getting the required paperwork completed so a young couple can receive a green light on the loan.

A loan officer who only sees the job as "pushing paper" or checking off one of many boxes on the required documents checklist is not likely to embrace the roller coaster of emotions that may be experienced by the couple as they seek approval on this loan.

But in applying the Head-Heart Connection, the loan officer will understand the higher purpose of the work is to make life better for the couple. By doing so, the loan officer will be *inspired* to provide more empathic support as the young couple navigates this very personal journey to buy a particular house that will become their family's first home. The loan officer will also look for opportunities to help the couple manage their fear and anxiety as they traverse the ups and downs of making the single, most expensive purchase of their lifetime. And the loan officer will celebrate with the couple when their loan is approved.

Which loan officer would make life better for this young couple? Which loan officer would you want to have taking care of your family member? Easy answer? Of course it is!

Ask yourself: Does your team really understand *why* you are in business and *what* impact you aspire to have on your customers?

The "Five Whys"
I'd like to suggest a simple tool you and your team can use to discover the Head-Heart Connection within your business. It's called the "Five Whys".

The "Five Whys" technique was formally developed by Sakichi Toyoda and was used within the Toyota Motor Corporation during the evolution of its manufacturing methodologies. This technique explores the cause-and-effect relationship of any problem or issue and has been broadly published and widely utilized within Six Sigma circles. While the technique is typically used to identify the root cause or a problem by repeating the question "Why?" five times, this approach can easily be used to help you and your employees understand the Head-Heart Connection within your business and to identify the big picture impact your organization is having on your customers.

I recently had a conversation with a partner and director of a large accounting firm. I was chatting with this CPA about the importance of employees having a clear line of sight between what they do every day and the organization's mission. I was intrigued and delighted when she shared the following insights. I have taken the liberty of including within the CPA's comments a hypothetical "Five Whys" conversation that could have guided the thought process to uncover the Head-Heart Connection for this organization.

CPA: What I do as a CPA is so much more than providing financial documents to my clients. I consider myself to be their trusted advisor.

Facilitator: *Why do you want to be your clients' trusted advisor?*

CPA: I need to help my clients understand what their financial documents mean.

Facilitator: *Why do you need to help your clients understand what their financial documents mean?*

CPA: If my clients understand what their financial documents mean, I can help them explore how they can increase their cash flow.

Facilitator: *Why do your clients need to explore how they can increase their cash flow?*

CPA: By increasing their cash flow, my clients can pay off debts or invest in necessary capital expenditures.

Facilitator: *Why* is it important your clients pay off debts or invest in necessary capital equipment?

CPA: By reducing their debt or investing in necessary capital equipment, they can provide better salaries and/or benefits to their employees.

Facilitator: *Why* is it important for your clients to provide better salaries or benefits to their employees?

CPA: When my clients invest in their people or in the growth of their businesses, the quality of life and the strength of our economy can be improved.

At the end of the day, what I really do is to *create an impact that will last a lifetime.*

Wow!

Some CPAs may tell you they simply prepare financial documents. This CPA really understands the Head-Heart Connection because she knows the true purpose of her team's work on the lives of her clients and her community.

No doubt the employees who work with this CPA will be inspired because they are making an impact that lasts a lifetime as opposed to merely producing financial documents.

In the Conversation Starters that follow this chapter, you will have an opportunity to use the "Five Whys" technique to help you and your employees embrace the Head-Heart Connection within your organization and understand the true impact your team is having on your customers.

Why is the "Five Whys" exercise important? Through understanding the real impact of your work, you and your team can quickly get to the heart of the matter!

Finding the Good in Bad

From tragedy to triumph, the Head-Heart Connection allowed me to discover good things can come from bad situations. Within a relatively short span of time, and in the midst of the heart-breaking death of my baby, I was equipped to move on, to seek and to seize the opportunity to pour my heart into an industry I have now loved for more than three decades.

Without question, it was the Head-Heart Connection that led those hospital employees at North Mississippi Medical Center to carry me through my time of deepest despair. I'm sure their job descriptions required them to meet my physical needs, but these people did so much more than that. Because they approached their work with their heads *and* with their hearts, they cared for me like I was the only person in their world. In so doing, they forever changed my life.

Through their acts of grace and goodness, these employees set the stage for me to join them in their caring profession as I was *called* to lead like I had never led before. From that day forward, I chose my own Option (C) as I would purposefully lead with my head and with my heart!

Conversation Starters for Your Team

1. Use the "Five Whys" technique to facilitate a conversation with your team regarding the Head-Heart Connection within your organization. What conclusion did your employees draw regarding the true impact of your team's work upon those individuals who are served by your organization?

2. What steps will you take to assure that your team understands they are doing meaningful work every day?

3. As a leader, what will you do differently to reinforce your team's efforts to make a positive difference every day for your customers?

4. What ideas do you have for inspiring your team members to view their work as more than "just a job"? What steps will you take to implement these ideas?

Notes

Gracious Leadership represents the intersection of ultimate respect and optimal outcomes.

Chapter 4

An Untraditional Career Path

O ther than my four-and-a-half years in banking, I essentially "grew up" within the healthcare industry. My professional journey in this space has been fascinating, to say the least, as I have worked for four very different healthcare systems.

North Mississippi Health Services (NMHS) is a multi-hospital, fully integrated healthcare delivery system based out of Tupelo, Mississippi. At the time of my service with this organization, NMMC (the flagship hospital of NMHS) was the largest medical center in the nation outside a Metropolitan Statistical Area.

Vanderbilt University Medical Center (VUMC) in Nashville, Tennessee, is one of the nation's most prestigious academic medical centers. VUMC's mission is to advance health and wellness through preeminent programs in patient care, education, and research.

Shands Healthcare (now known as University of Florida Health Shands Hospital) is based out of Gainesville, Florida. Shands has a close affiliation with a public university though the UF Health Science

Center and includes two large teaching hospitals, along with several other hospitals and facilities in North Florida.

Mount Carmel Health System (MCHS) is based out of Columbus, Ohio. MCHS is a faith-based, multi-hospital, fully-integrated healthcare delivery system that is a member of Trinity Health, the nation's second-largest Catholic healthcare system.

I was grateful for the opportunity to work for each of these fine organizations. Because of their diverse missions and unique cultures, these four healthcare systems provided fertile ground for abundant learning about leadership and life.

Throughout my healthcare career, I have held responsibility for disciplines such as strategy, business development, growth, physician integration, sales and marketing, public relations, and communications. Although I had gained ample operations experience within these areas during my first 20 years in healthcare, *hospital operations* had not been part of my assignments.

Even in the absence of this experience, I had long been encouraged by my mentors to seek an opportunity to lead a hospital. While this aspiration became one of my long-term goals, I frankly did not see my dream as realistically being within reach, particularly given that I had not followed the traditional career path of most healthcare CEOs and COOs. Yet, my trusted mentors continued to encourage me to pursue this C-Suite role for two primary reasons.

First, it was well known that I really liked to work with physicians. As odd as it may sound, having an affinity for working with doctors is not always the case for healthcare administrators. In fact, I once served with a colleague who did not at all like working with doctors. And he wasn't shy about sharing his sentiments. He definitely was not on the physicians' "best friends at work" list!

I figured out on my first day on the job in healthcare administration in 1983 that healthcare executives don't admit patients to hospitals … doctors do! As such, I quickly learned that physicians should be viewed both as customers and as partners. Physician relationship management became second nature to me, and physician relationship management strategies became a non-negotiable part of my teams' ongoing objectives.

Second, along the way I had become known as a leader who appreciated the contributions of all members of my teams. Employee engagement scores were high, and with very rare exception, my employees were happy. They delivered great results, as they were inspired to contribute to our higher calling of serving those who most needed us.

Seize the Moment

In the fall of 2004, I was approached about relocating to Columbus, Ohio, to serve as senior vice president of corporate development for Mount Carmel Health System.

While the role I was being recruited to assume at Mount Carmel was well within my traditional career path, I thought this specific recruitment opportunity provided a prime time for me to make an "ask" regarding my long-standing dream to lead a hospital.

I had nothing to lose.

I told the CEO I would move to Columbus and lead the corporate development division if he would promise I could run one of the hospitals as future opportunities arose.

The CEO agreed, and I made the move to the Buckeye State.

Approximately 18 months after relocating, I was given the opportunity to lead Mount Carmel St. Ann's Hospital (MCSA). My professional dream had come true as I was given the most important stretch assignment of my life.

For this incredible opportunity, I want to acknowledge one of my favorite leaders, Mike Slubowski, currently the President and Chief Operating Officer of Trinity Health.

Mr. Slubowski is the executive who took a chance by allowing me to lead a hospital when I previously had no experience in hospital operations.

For many years, I have admired Mr. Slubowski as an exceptional leader. He sets the bar high for extraordinary performance from himself and those who follow him.

He positions his leaders for success, supports them to assure they have an opportunity to excel, and leads in a soulful, respectful manner.

For the confidence and faith that Mr. Slubowski placed in me, I shall forever be grateful.

And, of course, I happily accepted the offer to lead MCSA.

Be Careful What You Ask For
The hospital for which I was assuming operational responsibility had a rich history and heritage, having been founded in 1908 by the Sisters of St. Francis of Stella Niagara, New York.

Initially serving as an infant asylum (orphanage) and a home for unwed mothers in and around Columbus, Ohio, St. Ann's started providing maternity services in 1920 and subsequently became a women's hospital. Only in 1972 did St. Ann's accept its first male patient. The hospital relocated to Westerville in 1984, and in 1995, was purchased by Mount Carmel Health System.

The people of St. Ann's had great pride in their independent spirit and reputation for having a culture of compassion. In the Columbus metropolitan market, St. Ann's was also well known as a great place to have a baby.

Prior to my going to MCSA, I was pleased to learn about this hospital's rich history, its campus pride, and compassionate culture. It was also my understanding that the hospital had a significant opportunity for improvement in its financial performance. Just prior to my arrival, the campus had experienced some degree of trauma which would require special attention to solidify a foundation of trust.

As I began my work, I quickly learned that while the employees were indeed compassionate, inconsistencies existed in employee accountability. Hardworking employees were openly and freely asking that leadership start requiring *all* employees to carry their fair share of the workload. Early conversations with physicians also indicated that a more purposeful and accountable focus was needed on the quality of care.

Not long after this, the public reporting of patient satisfaction scores was initiated by the federal government. Our leaders and staff received jolting news as our hospital's patient satisfaction scores from a prior year appeared in the regional newspaper. The story in the *Columbus Dispatch* stated the stark reality that MCSA had the lowest patient satisfaction scores of any hospital in central Ohio.

Needless to say, in the midst of my dream to lead a hospital, I found myself at the helm of an organization with very tall mountains to climb. In fact, to reach peak performance we needed a full organizational turnaround. Had my "dream come true" to lead a hospital morphed into a nightmare?

Where do you start in leading the necessary course corrections? And, how in the world do you approach such challenges?

I didn't know the answers, but I did know that our team at MCSA would need to *lead like we had never led before.*

Our Leadership Team would need to inspire our staff to embrace the Head-Heart Connection and focus on treating every patient like the *only* person in our world ... just as those employees at NMMC had done for me during my point of greatest need.

To serve our patients and our community in the best manner possible, our Leadership Team embarked upon a most challenging journey to our coveted mountaintop. And together we sought to reach peak performance by improving our results across our balanced scorecard.

We recognized that to reach this summit, we would need to believe that we could become a destination hospital where employees, physicians, and volunteers would aspire to work, and where patients would readily want to come for their care.

I knew as the leader of this hospital with very tall mountains to climb, I would need to role model the most impactful and positive principles of leadership ... Gracious Leadership ... which I had learned throughout my life. I believed with my head and with my heart that Gracious Leadership would be the best way to get our team to peak performance.

Why?

Because Gracious Leadership represents the intersection of ultimate respect and optimal outcomes. And it was precisely this type of unique approach that would be required.

PART II

THE KEY INGREDIENTS OF GRACIOUS LEADERSHIP

No leader can optimally lead his or her organization to achieve its full potential unless every person in every role feels respected, valued, and appreciated.

Chapter 5

Gracious Leaders are Respectful

G racious leaders are respectful to every person regardless of their role, title, or position. My conviction about this principle came from my parents, who openly and freely believed all people were created equally.

My father and mother lived this conviction during the Civil Rights Movement in the 1960s. In fact, my father was well ahead of his time as he advocated for Equal Rights in my home state of Mississippi at a point in history when supporting equality for all people was *not at all popular.*

My father would absolutely bristle if he saw other people "putting on airs" or "putting down others" for any reason, including their race or economic status. He abhorred pretense and felt leaders should be down to earth and relatable. My father taught my brother and me that because all people are to be fully respected, leaders must always do what's right to assure fair treatment for every individual, even and especially when it's not easy.

I am extraordinarily grateful for the fundamental lessons of respect I learned from my parents. These life lessons built the foundation for me as a leader to appreciate the value brought forth by *every* team member, regardless of their position. From housekeeper to physician, my parents taught me by example that every person is fearfully and wonderfully made in the eyes of God (Psalms 139:14).

As such, I have come to believe that no leader, regardless of impressive title, can *optimally lead* his or her organization to achieve its full potential unless *every* person in *every* role feels respected, valued, and appreciated.

The Welcome Gift
When I went to MCSA in the summer of 2006, I had no idea that during my first week I would be faced with an unexpected moment of truth. I had literally been on the campus no more than three days when the environmental services manager asked to meet with me.

I expected this might be an introductory conversation.

I was wrong.

The manager wanted to make me aware that an external consultant who was working with her staff had been belittling and threatening to her employees. The manager clearly didn't agree with his heavy-handed approach, and she wanted to communicate her concern about the situation.

I thanked her for bringing the issue to my attention and promised to follow up with her upon learning more.

With only two phone calls—and as many emails—I confirmed her story. I also quickly discovered the disappointing information she shared was just the tip of the iceberg.

In the midst of the disrespectful comments the consultant had told these front-line employees, he also boasted that if they did not do as he had instructed, *"Janet Meeks would have them fired."*

Are you kidding me? Not good.

In that moment, I made one phone call to the president of the consulting firm. On the spot, I fired the egregious consultant and told the president of the company the consultant had to leave our organization immediately. Furthermore, I communicated that he was *not* to return to our campus.

I shared our expectation that *all* our employees would be treated with utmost respect and any person who made threats or disrespectful comments to our staff would not be welcomed on our campus.

Little did I know at the time the magnitude of the *gift* brought forth by our environmental services manager. I am deeply grateful she had the courage to voice her grave concern to a new leader whom she had not yet met.

My "in the moment" decision to remove the egregious consultant quickly sent positive shock waves throughout the hospital. The word spread quickly that at our hospital every person would be treated with respect. Period. No exceptions.

This unplanned action set the stage for creating a culture of consistent respect for the 1,900 employees, 700 physicians, 300 volunteers on our campus, and, of course, our patients.

Only when an organization's culture is grounded in respect can sustained success be achieved in an optimal manner.

Walk a Mile in My Shoes

One approach I have used to show my respect for staff is to spend time periodically shadowing employees and physicians ... literally to walk a mile in their shoes and role model respect for the staff at all levels.

Whether I was shadowing housekeepers, surgeons, physical therapists, nurses, techs, third-shift emergency physicians, or others, I always learned more about the challenges our staff faced through spending time with them and following in their footsteps.

The shadowing experiences gave me an opportunity to understand what their days were like and take action, whenever possible, to address the frustrations, as well as the opportunities, these individuals encountered. Through shadowing, my goal was to seek ways to empathize with our staff at all levels and identify ways we might become an even better place to work.

I shall never forget one of my shadowing experiences with our food and nutrition services (FNS) staff at MCSA. As I was helping an employee unload the commercial dishwasher in our hospital's kitchen, I noticed a whirlwind of activity at the patient tray assembly line. The employees were working in a very small space. They were rapidly preparing the patient food trays as the conveyor belt progressively moved each tray down the line.

This observation gave me a momentary flashback to the *I Love Lucy* television series that I watched as a child. In particular, I thought about Lucy's famous chocolate scene, in which Lucy and Ethel were working on the assembly line in a candy factory. As they were assembling the chocolates, the conveyor belt began to run faster and faster. Poor Lucy and Ethel couldn't keep up, and they started devouring the chocolates and stuffing them into their uniforms and hats to avoid any appearance of "waste."

Now, while the conveyor belt at MCSA was functioning properly, it was crystal clear that our FNS employees needed more space to do their work well.

Observations from this shadowing experience led me to ask more questions about our kitchen facilities, which had been built when the hospital relocated to Westerville in 1984. At the time of relocation, MCSA had 90 inpatient beds. With the campus expansion that we were already planning, the hospital would soon have 330 beds. Clearly more space was needed to provide top-notch food service to our patients and assure a pleasant work environment for our employees.

We subsequently made an ask to corporate leadership for the capital required to expand our kitchen and dining facilities. The request was approved, and we celebrated, knowing that soon the space for our kitchen and dining facilities would be tripled in size.

One of my favorite memories from MCSA was the day our new kitchen and dining facilities were debuted for our FNS staff. These employees had been amazing troopers as they had endured significant inconvenience during the construction process.

When the building project was completed, a "Thank You" luncheon was held for the FNS staff. Immediately following this celebratory gathering, our Leadership Team lined the corridors between the location of the luncheon and the "soon to be revealed" state-of-the-art dining facilities.

Our leaders gave this team resounding applause and abundant high fives. Many of these front-line employees had broad, beaming smiles; others had tears of joy streaming down their faces. It was quite a sight to experience their wide eyes of amazement and awe as they walked into Bryden Bistro for the first time!

Without having had the shadowing opportunity to "walk a mile in the shoes" of our FNS employees, I would not have obtained the first-hand knowledge and resulting empathy to appreciate what I needed to do as a leader to advocate for this important facilities expansion.

Shadowing is just one of many ways you can show respect to your team. Seeking to empathize with your staff, understand more about their work life, and make their work life better can certainly help your employees feel respected.

A leader can also show respect by expressing gratitude or seeking input from employees at all levels of the organization. We will cover these topics in Chapters 14 and 17. But respect absolutely must be at the foundation of an organization, just as physiological needs are at the base of Maslow's Hierarchy of Needs. And, as my parents taught me when I was a young child, gracious leaders show uncompromising respect to all and expect the same *from* all *to* all.

Conversation Starters for Your Team

1. What specific actions will you take to assure that your direct reports feel they are fully respected?

2. What specific steps will your team take to show that employees at all levels of your organization are respected?

3. If you were the CEO of your organization, what one thing would you do differently to help your organization's employees at all levels feel they are fully respected?

A trust-based common bond will allow your team to focus on what matters most... delighting your customers by achieving the right results through the right relationships.

Chapter 6

Gracious Leaders Value Relationships

I n today's fast-paced corporate environment, the heat is on for leaders to deliver value and prove their worth to their respective organizations.

As leaders are recruited to *new* organizations or as leaders are promoted within existing corporations, one of the most common mistakes they can make is to act too quickly. It's easy to do. As a newcomer with fresh eyes, you can immediately see where changes are needed—and you want to act!

The low hanging fruit is ready for the harvest. You want to demonstrate in short order you are rapidly making necessary changes your new boss described during your interview process. You *feel* the pressure to act. You're *challenged* to achieve greater results within shorter spans of time and with fewer resources. The bar is constantly set higher to do more with less. Achieve more and do it now!

In such circumstances, it is easy for a new leader to get caught up in this urgency to act. I experienced such a situation when I fell short in appreciating the fact that relationships must be a top priority *before* necessary advancements can be realized in an *optimal* manner. Particularly when a change agenda is in the wind, gracious leaders should embrace the strategic importance of forging relationships of trust with key stakeholders. Failure to do so can result in the tragic derailment of an executive's career.

I learned firsthand that *positive relationships will precede positive outcomes.* And when positive relationships are sincerely established, trust and engagement follow. It is at this juncture that the stage is better set for the change necessary to advance an organization. Gracious leaders are wise enough to know when relationships are Job No. 1, optimal results can be achieved more quickly. Although it sounds counterintuitive, sometimes as a leader you simply must slow down before you can speed up.

Slow Down Before You Speed Up
There was a specific time in my professional journey when I painfully learned the importance of slowing down before I could speed up.

I had been named to a senior leadership role within a multi-billion-dollar healthcare system and was recruited to lead the implementation of a new strategic plan. It was clear one of the departments for which I was responsible needed to improve its performance. The quality of this department's work product was not up to par, and the department's leaders did not realize the deficiencies because the approach and output had been acceptable within the organization for years. In short, with great intentions, the department's employees were busy producing work that was nice but not strategic.

With fresh eyes, I saw the changes required to accomplish the desired advances. Departmental goals needed to be clearly defined so performance could be measured against prescribed results. The staff would need to assure an acceptable return on investment for its expenditures. And a long-time, beloved vendor did not have the strategic horsepower to support this department.

Even though I could see the need for specific change, some of the tenured employees were perfectly content with the way things were. In fact, they considered it an insult that any newcomer might think they needed change. They weren't interested in having some newbie, regardless of title, telling them the way they were doing things was not good enough.

So what happened?

They stalled, and so also did my aspirations to see rapid improvement in performance.

It was suggested by a colleague that I needed to slow down and get to know the staff *before* trying to affect the needed changes.

Relationships Matter

Slow down? I don't think so! As a Type A personality, the thought of slowing down did not sound like a viable option. And besides, every day we were missing out on significant opportunities.

It was at this juncture that I learned one of the most important leadership lessons of my professional life. To be successful, I did indeed have to slow down purposefully and build relationships of trust. Only then, could I speed up and lead the change required to optimize performance.

I heeded my co-worker's advice. I spent time with the employees in that department and learned more about their long-standing love of their organization and how close they were as professional colleagues. For some of the staff, this was the only place they had ever worked. Their co-workers were their life friends. Most importantly, I learned how proud they were of their work.

This knowledge of their passions provided me with much needed insight. It served as a baseline of understanding from which we could build a plan for achieving the right results at the right time and in the right manner. *Together* we dreamt big and set the bar high for the future performance of the department. The staff began to develop an understanding of *why* we needed to pursue our work differently, not as criticism of their past efforts, but rather in being more strategic as we worked towards peak performance.

Without too much time passing, the staff became excited about the enhanced approaches to their work. They also took great pride in the fresh and outstanding products they had begun to deliver.

Slow down to speed up? As perplexing as it may sound, it's well worth the effort. And while establishing solid relationships does not have to take a lot of time, it does require being purposeful and, most importantly, being sincere.

With solid relationships at the foundation of your leadership platform, you should be better equipped to lead your team to achieve more with less, faster than ever!

Getting It Right from the Start

As a leader, I love continuous learning, including the difficult lessons I have gleaned from the proverbial "School of Hard Knocks." After I understood firsthand the importance of slowing down before speeding up, I made it my practice to be purposeful and systematic in building relationships early on with all key stakeholders.

By demonstrating a genuine interest in getting to know your employees, gracious leaders can quickly establish relationships grounded in trust. Sincerity is vital, however, as employees can sense a disingenuous spirit from a mile away.

In addition to the approach I described in Chapter 2 as I was getting acquainted with my new coworkers at North Mississippi Medical Center, I became purposeful and strategic about conversations with new employees during their formal orientation process.

In interactions with new employees, I like to pose the following questions:

- What is your new role?

- Which department will be your home?

- Why did you want to work here?

Many times, I have heard employees convey that a family member or a friend referred them because they loved our organization's culture and encouraged them to apply. Of course, it was great for other new employees to hear the accolades that our organization was a wonderful place to work.

Some newcomers shared about a personal health experience that made them want to pay forward the kindness that had been extended to them or a family member when they were ill or injured.

Such stories gave us an opportunity to emphasize our conviction that each and every employee's role was important in every customer's experience. We reinforced to them we were counting on each of them and needed them to do their part so our organization would continue to be a great place to work and an excellent place for patients to come for care.

Lastly, we asked the question, "What do you *love* to do when you are not at work?"

With rare exception, we saw smiles of delight when we posed this unexpected question.

Employees spoke with pride about their children or grandchildren. Some shared about their hobbies, such as playing in a rock band, jogging, or traveling. Others talked about their love of reading and favorite books.

A few new employees actually laughed as they shared how much they enjoyed getting to sleep. And what's not to love about a good night's sleep!?!

Creating Trust Through Caring

Why were these questions important? Employees want to know their leaders are down to earth, relatable, and approachable. They want to know their employer really cares about every employee as a whole person and not just for what he or she does while at work. Employees also want to know their leaders are genuinely and sincerely interested in how every employee contributes to the organization's success.

Employees will likely spend more of their waking hours at work than they spend at home with their families. Because of this reality, I have always wanted my employees to feel "at home" while they are at work.

When gracious leaders take the time to know their employees from the beginning, they can help to minimize the "We-They" mentality and mobilize an energized team imbued with the potential to reach peak performance.

The presence of a trust-based, common bond will allow your team to focus on what matters most ... delighting your customers by achieving the right results through the right relationships!

Gracious leaders are purposeful in helping all employees know their leaders really do care about them as whole people. And gracious leaders understand that positive relationships are required to achieve optimal outcomes.

Conversation Starters for Your Team

1. Think about the quality of the relationships that you have with your direct reports. What steps will you take to improve the quality of those relationships?

2. Describe your perception of the quality of the relationships that exist among your direct reports. Then ask your direct reports to describe the quality of relationships that exist among the members of their team. What steps will you take to facilitate any opportunities for improvement in those relationships?

3. What specific actions will you take to build relationships of trust with every employee and minimize any "We-They" mentality that may exist between your organization's leadership and the employees?

4. If you were the CEO of your organization, what specific actions would you take to assure that relationships of trust exist between your leaders and your frontline employees?

Listen like the other person is the *only* person in your world.

Chapter 7

Gracious Leaders Listen with Purpose and Respond with Care

T he ability to communicate effectively is an absolute "must have" in your leadership tool kit. My favorite definition of communications is "to listen and to talk." I've always believed that the person who does the most talking during a conversation will feel better about the discussion when it's over. However, the person who listens most will be more enlightened at the end of the dialogue.

God gave us two ears and one mouth for a reason. Just imagine how much better our relationships would be at home and work if we devoted twice as much time to listening to the views of others as opposed to dwelling on voicing our own positions. Think about it!

Effective listening with purpose requires discipline, focus, and selflessness.

- Discipline is needed so we can train ourselves to hold back and hear what the other person wants to share. This can be a challenge, as leaders aspire to make things better for their teams "in the moment." Leaders like to fix things that are broken. And we like to provide quick answers to facilitate expeditious problem resolution.

- Focus is required so we can concentrate on capturing the details of the story the other person wants us to hear as opposed to *pretending* to listen while we are thinking about the next comments we will make.

- Selflessness is shown when we let the other person be the center of the conversation. In so doing, we demonstrate respect so the other individual feels he or she has been heard.

When leaders use discipline, focus, and selflessness as the foundation of listening with purpose, the other person will not only feel valued, but will also be more inclined to embrace the leader's vision for the organization's future.

Listen Like the Other Person is the *Only* Person in Your World
While I worked at Vanderbilt University Medical Center, I had the great pleasure of serving under the leadership of Dr. Harry R. Jacobson, who at the time was the vice chancellor for health affairs at Vanderbilt University and the CEO of Vanderbilt University Medical Center. Dr. Jacobson is the co-founder and partner of TriStar Health Partners.

Although I'm not sure that he realized it, Dr. Jacobson was one of the best listeners I have ever encountered in my professional life. He had the Midas touch and brought an entrepreneurial spirit into academia that was refreshing, exciting, and inspiring. Dr. Jacobson was one very busy, very successful leader. Yet I was always taken with how he intentionally and carefully listened to others with great purpose.

As an example, I recall observing Dr. Jacobson's listening skills in action during our weekly Clinical Enterprise Group Meetings (senior leadership team meetings). He demonstrated profound respect for presenters as he absorbed the "what," the "why," and the "how" of the material shared. Dr. Jacobson held back in offering comments until the presenters' stories were shared. Then, in the spirit of the academic debate, he would pose powerful questions that would guide the presenters to contemplate ways through which they could further strengthen their proposals.

Through being fully present, maintaining eye contact, and avoiding distractions such as cell phones or other interruptions, Dr. Jacobson showed great respect for his followers by epitomizing the discipline, focus, and selflessness required for leaders to listen with purpose.

Even though Dr. Jacobson likely had myriad issues or opportunities flowing through his brilliant mind at any given moment, when I was in a conversation with him, I always felt he sincerely wanted to hear what I was expressing.

I had a profound light bulb moment the day I realized that Dr. Jacobson listened to me like I was the *only* person in his world. Just as the hospital employees at North Mississippi Medical Center had made me feel like the *only* person in their world, this outstanding physician leader had accomplished the very same thing.

By listening with purpose and clinging onto every word that I shared, Dr. Jacobson made me feel valued, respected, and heard.

Just imagine the potential positive impact on *all* of our relationships … at work … at home … throughout our communities and beyond … if only we all would listen as though the other person was the *only* person in our world.

When Technology Gets in the Way

We live in an era in which technology has become the most prevalent mode of communications.

Believe me, I love my smart phone as much as anyone. Yet so much of our ability to communicate effectively can be lost if we no longer listen with our ears *and* with our hearts.

Think about your own co-workers or your family. How much of your time is spent captive to a piece of technology as opposed to really *being* together and fully present?

And how much of our workforce efficiency is lost when employees and leaders are glued to their cell phones as opposed to focusing on the tasks they are to perform?

I was talking recently with a colleague who is a partner in a highly regarded, global professional services organization. She shared that she recently had two interns who were very bright but not getting their work done well because they each were constantly distracted by their cell phones. Because the interns did not respond to the feedback provided to them regarding their suboptimal performance associated with phone distractions, the firm made a decision not to retain them. Such a decision was a clear departure from the norm for this organization, as its leaders strive to retain its interns. The careers of these two young people were derailed early on because of an inappropriate dependency upon technology.

As leaders, we must be aware of the dangerous barriers to effective communications, productivity, and positive relationships that can be present when we become servant to our technological resources.

I'm not inferring that communicating with technology is bad. Much to the contrary, technology has given us revolutionary options for faster communications with a broader audience and less cost.

What I am saying, however, is that we cannot let technology get in the way of delivering the right message in the right manner. As leaders, we must be aware of the potential to usurp the relationships that matter most to us at work or at home when we let the use of technology replace listening with our ears and with our hearts.

Listening with Purpose in Organizations of All Sizes

Depending upon the size of your organization, you may find it helpful to implement systematic listening processes so that as a gracious leader, you can become more strategic about listening with purpose.

Throughout my career, I have utilized a variety of listening venues for employees, physicians, customers, and other key stakeholders. Why? Because with large numbers of employees and physicians who work in hospitals and health systems on a 24/7/365 basis, we needed multiple approaches through which we could communicate frequently, thoroughly, and effectively.

And we wanted our most important stakeholders to feel valued, appreciated, and heard. We believed that happy employees should lead to happy patients, and physicians should be viewed both as our partners and our customers. We also found great value in asking our customers to tell us how we could improve.

As such, in addition to staff and leadership meetings, I have held 'Round-the-Clock' town hall meetings for employees and round table conversations for physicians and other key stakeholders, such as major employers.

Depending upon the particular challenges we faced, or the specific opportunities we were embracing, these listening sessions were held in various formats and sizes. Some sessions were small and more intimate, like a fireside chat. Others might include several hundred participants at a time with more formal presentations along with a designated time for Q&A.

Regardless of the format, the goal of the listening sessions was to open the door for meaningful conversations with our key stakeholders. We wanted to listen with purpose for issues that needed to be resolved or for opportunities that could be pursued.

Three Powerful Questions

With organizations of all sizes, you can achieve great results through using the following three powerful questions in your listening venues.

- What one thing should we do to make our customers' experience better?

- What one thing should we change to make your work life better?

- Is there anything else that you'd like to discuss?

These three simple, yet profound, questions have served me well as they have opened the doors widely for feedback. Three powerful questions have helped to set the stage that we would be a listening leadership team that sincerely wanted to hear the opinions from the front line and from customers regarding how we could continuously improve.

I'd like to share a quick heads up: As you start purposeful listening sessions with your employees or other key stakeholders, don't be surprised if you initially hear significant griping and complaining. It can feel like you're going to a fire hydrant for a sip of water. Complaints can vary wildly from dissatisfaction with pay, benefits, the dress code, or the quality of food in the cafeteria all the way to the perception that overtime is not equitably distributed or that some co-workers had been receiving preferential treatment.

Regardless of the nature of the complaints, it is important to be patient in understanding that the release of pent up frustrations can be liberating for your staff and your organization. And hearing freely-shared concerns early on can help you quickly get to the root cause of the issues that, as distractions, may be preventing your team from realizing its full potential.

Hearing complaints with patience also allows you to listen for themes as you discern the difference between legitimate concerns of loyal employees versus mere griping on the part of naysayers.

Listening with purpose takes time, but after all, it is our time that is the most important gift we will ever share with others.

Responding with Care

Gracious leaders listen with purpose, and they respond with care. Responding with care requires patience and self-restraint to create a work environment in which people feel they can speak up safely, they are heard, and, therefore, their feedback is valued.

As counterintuitive as it may feel, employees are actually paying leaders a great compliment when they are comfortable enough to share their complaints and concerns directly as opposed to anonymously. When employees share concerns directly with the leader, they believe the leader cares enough to hear the feedback, to honor that feedback, and to address legitimate concerns without retribution.

When a leader asks for feedback, it is important to refrain from shutting down the feedback or openly discounting the comments. That being said, if the information shared is not factual, the leader needs to set the record straight respectfully, with facts.

Gracious leaders understand that legitimate concerns represent opportunities for improvement and that problems are to be viewed as gifts. I'll share more on this topic in Chapter 8.

Complaining Can Require Courage

In cultures where leaders are not readily open to hearing concerns, employees can be afraid to speak up because they fear retribution from management or even from their peers. Such cultures are not healthy, nor can they be maximally productive, as unaddressed, small issues can accumulate and ultimately show up as major problems that are difficult to correct.

I have experienced an unhealthy organizational culture in which employees were not open about their concerns because they were afraid they would get in trouble with "someone" if they voiced their complaints. Regrettably this appears to be more common in Corporate America than we might care to admit.

I have also experienced a corporate culture in which employees were not only enthusiastically encouraged to speak up systematically about real or perceived issues, but they were also recognized and praised for reporting legitimate concerns that needed to be addressed. This type of healthy culture speaks volumes about the level of trust that exists between the leadership of the company and its employees.

Gracious leaders understand that employees and other key stakeholders who are closest to the customers are the ones with the best view of their reality. The employees on the front line are well equipped to understand what is working correctly and which easy-to-fix broken processes are causing daily frustrations that impede their efficiency or customer satisfaction.

Gracious leaders encourage employees to be courageous by speaking up openly and honestly about legitimate concerns. Just know that those employees who do speak up for the benefit of the organization are demonstrating implicit trust in their leaders.

Silence is Not Golden

Some leaders believe that silence is golden, and those who complain are nothing more than whiners. However, many "Silence is Golden" leaders are missing out on the organization's most impactful opportunities for improvement.

Why?

Because as leaders, we can only fix what's broken if we know about it.

Gracious leaders therefore listen with purpose so they can understand the issues that need to be addressed. And gracious leaders respond with care so they can continuously keep the doors open to hear additional opportunities for improvement.

Unvoiced concerns, small or large, can snowball into major issues that may have expensive and long-lasting, negative repercussions. As such, gracious leaders should view legitimately expressed concerns as gifts that can lead to continuous improvement and a highly productive, engaged workforce.

Thank, Act, Communicate Action, and Thank Again

Whether leaders are asking for feedback from their direct reports, the front line, customers, or other key stakeholders, when hearing the feedback (be it positive or negative), the first response from the gracious leader should be "Thank you" ... not "OMG" or "That's not true."

The following steps should be taken:

- **THANK:** Express gratitude to the individual for bringing the matter to your attention. Share that you appreciate knowing about the concern because you can only fix what's broken if you know about it.

- **ACT:** Take action to address the situation.

- **COMMUNICATE ACTION:** Communicate the action that was taken (or, if action could not be taken, explain why not).

- **THANK AGAIN:** Thank the person again when you tell the individual that action has been taken.

Before you think, "Duh! That's common sense," be aware this approach is not as commonly used as you might think.

A Problem Can Still Exist After Being Addressed

Even though a leader addresses a problem, unless the leader responds with care by purposefully communicating the action that was taken, the person who provided the feedback may believe no action was taken at all. In these circumstances, the individual may feel devalued or, worse, that the leader doesn't care.

I recall a situation in which a physician shared with me a concern. I asked the affected manager to address the issue, and she committed to do so promptly.

The physician and I crossed paths a few weeks later and, expecting that the manager had quickly addressed the problem, I confidently asked the physician if we had addressed the issue to his satisfaction.

He said, "No."

This was embarrassing, to say the least. After apologizing for this faux pas, I promised to follow up promptly.

When I called the manager to inquire as to why the concern had not been addressed, she was surprised. She shared that she had indeed addressed the issue the same day the physician had brought the matter to our attention.

I then asked the manager if she had closed the loop with the physician, and she quietly said, "No."

You see, to this physician, the problem had not been addressed because we didn't tell him we had fixed the concern that was important to him.

Gracious leaders listen with purpose, and they respond with care. And they care enough to close the loop with those who bring forth the gift of feedback.

Conversation Starters for Your Team

1. Consider how well you currently *listen with purpose* within your organization. What will you do differently to ensure you are more purposeful as you listen to others?

2. Consider how well the leaders of your organization listen with purpose to all of their employees. What specific steps will you take to ensure the leaders of your organization will be more effective in listening with purpose?

3. In what ways do you consistently demonstrate that you *respond with care* to your employees? What will you do differently to ensure you are more effective in consistently responding with care?

4. How do the leaders of your organization consistently demonstrate they are responding with care to their employees? What specific steps will you take to ensure your leaders will be more effective in responding with care?

5. What steps will you take to encourage your organization's employees to be more courageous in offering candid feedback?

6. What steps will you take to ensure you and your leaders consistently close the loop with individuals who bring forth concerns?

Resolve complaints quickly so
you have the opportunity to
optimize customer loyalty and
minimize organizational risk.

Chapter 8

Gracious Leaders See Problems as Opportunities

Gracious leaders see problems as an opportunity to serve. The more problems we know about, the greater opportunities we will have to address the issues, make our products and services better for our customers, and improve our work environment for our employees.

One of my favorite books is *How to Win Customers and Keep Them for Life* by Michael LeBoeuf, Ph.D. The author says "Resolve a complaining customer's problem on the spot and the odds are 19-1 that he will do business with you again. Mishandle the complaint and you will lose him forever, not to mention the eight to 10 people he will tell."

Dr. LeBouef further shares, "A rapidly settled complaint can actually create more customer loyalty than would have been created if it had never occurred."

The author's findings underscore the strategic opportunity to view problems as gifts, resolve issues quickly, and communicate your actions as well as your gratitude to the individuals who brought forth the problems.

Problems Really Are an Opportunity to Serve

Gracious leaders are always on the lookout for ways through which their teams can better serve those who need them most. In asking employees for feedback, you may have to overcome cultural norms in which people do not speak up regarding concerns or suggestions.

Some organizations have an environment in which concerns, if reported at all, are conveyed anonymously. Anonymous hotlines are an important vehicle to have available when employees don't feel comfortable voicing concerns directly to their leaders. However, I believe such lines should not *replace* the need to foster a culture in which open and honest, direct feedback is readily provided by employees to leadership. One of the issues with anonymous feedback is that even if a problem has been corrected, you don't know whom to thank and with whom to communicate that the deficiency has been addressed.

Through adopting a leadership philosophy that openly and actively *celebrates* the reporting of concerns, your culture can be transformed into an environment in which problems are solved because they are reported, and innovation can more readily be achieved.

Gracious leaders seek to create a culture of transparency. They want employees to know with confidence that they will be praised openly for bringing forth concerns because their leaders are committed to view problems as opportunities to serve.

Ensure Rapid Complaint Resolution in Risk Mitigation

The rapid resolution of complaints is not only important in building employee and customer loyalty, but it is also vital in the mitigation of risk among internal and external customers.

Gracious leaders should be purposeful about teaching their leaders the critical importance of expeditious complaint management.

As Dr. LeBoeuf explained, the sooner a manager can respond to a complaint, the higher is the likelihood that the person who brought forth the complaint will be content with the resolution.

I shall never forget one situation in which several members of my team were scheduled to meet with two irate families. Each of the families had independently brought forth unrelated issues.

We entered each meeting well-prepared, with a commitment that we would listen with purpose and respond with care.

Each family shared their stories, and they certainly did not hold back as they needed to vent. They were *not* happy, to say the least, and they let us know it.

We listened carefully and patiently, avoiding any tendency to appear defensive. In such meetings, we learned important insights from our patients and their loved ones. We continuously wanted to find opportunities for improvement in the customers' perceptions as well as in their realities.

We thanked each of the families for their feedback. We expressed our sincere regret they had experienced disappointment. And we further told them the steps we had already taken to assure such situations might be avoided in the future.

At the conclusion of each meeting, the families expressed their gratitude that we took the time to meet with them. They actually seemed surprised that *someone* cared enough to listen.

They thanked us for appreciating their concerns and for responding in a manner in which they felt they had been sincerely heard. In situations in which their perceptions were not accurate, they thanked us for clarifying what had actually occurred.

Each family left after giving us hugs of gratitude.

Within a week, we received "Thank You" notes from each of these families.

Transformation had occurred (from irate customers to grateful and, hopefully, loyal customers) because our leaders viewed problems as opportunities for improvement.

What is the lesson here?

By viewing problems as opportunities to serve and improve, and by taking the time to resolve complaints quickly, gracious leaders within any industry have the opportunity to optimize customer loyalty and to minimize organizational risk.

Avoid the "Yes People" When Looking for Opportunities to Serve
In addition to seeking feedback from the front line, it is also imperative for leaders to surround themselves with direct reports who are trusted advisors. Professional relationships with direct reports should be so strong that these individuals will be uncompromisingly honest with their leaders about what is going well and what needs improvement.

Dan Wilford is the CEO who hired me for my first healthcare role at North Mississippi Medical Center. Mr. Wilford, now president emeritus of Memorial Hermann Healthcare System based out of Houston, Texas, is a revered icon among healthcare administrators nationwide.

Early in my tenure at NMMC, Mr. Wilford was a guest speaker at a conference I was attending. During the Q & A session, an attendee asked Mr. Wilford to describe what he expected from those who reported directly to him.

On the spot, he said, "I expect those who report to me to know more about their respective areas of responsibility than I do. Otherwise, why do I need them?"

Mr. Wilford's message was clear and on point. He sought to surround himself with individuals who were experts within their respective disciplines. I liked this approach and adopted it as one among many of the leadership principles I learned from this outstanding healthcare leader.

There is an additional expectation I have had for those individuals who report to me. As trite as it sounds, I only want to surround myself with people whom I can completely trust. An important part of this trust is an expectation that those who report to me will *always* tell me the truth, even if they think that it's something I don't want to hear.

There was no room in our C-Suite for "Yes People." They are a dime a dozen, and they are selfish, as their goal is to play it safe by avoiding potential offense to the boss.

I have always strived to surround myself with selfless direct reports who would tell me the unvarnished truth about how "I" and "We" could be better. These leaders joined me in the conviction that a problem is indeed an opportunity to serve.

Over the course of my career, I have found those individuals who were the most transparent with me, regardless of the circumstances, were the same employees whose growth and development I aspired to foster. It has been those leaders to whom I gave stretch assignments and whose names would show up during our succession planning conversations.

Gracious leaders see problems as opportunities to serve, and they look for such opportunities all the time ... all around them ... and also within themselves.

Conversation Starters for Your Team

1. Describe what your team is currently doing to demonstrate a consistent conviction that problems represent an opportunity to serve. What specific actions will you take to assure that you and your team consistently view problems as "gifts"?

2. What processes does your organization currently utilize to foster a culture of transparency in which employees are encouraged to report problems proactively? What specific steps will you take to encourage the proactive and transparent reporting of concerns?

3. Describe what your team is currently doing to demonstrate its commitment to the expeditious resolution of complaints. What specific steps will you take to affect improvements in your organization's complaint resolution processes?

4. What specific steps will you take to create a culture in which your staff tells you what you "need" to hear as opposed to what they think you "want" to hear?

5. If you were the CEO of your organization, what specific steps would you take to facilitate an open, transparent culture in which problems are viewed as an opportunity to serve?

Empower those who follow you
by teaching them to address their
own challenges.

Chapter 9

Gracious Leaders Ask the Right Questions

In leadership training, we often talk about the importance of delegation to our staff. But have you ever given much thought to the concept of *upward delegation*?

How many times has an employee entered your office and posed the following scenario?

"Here's a problem. What should we do?"

If you answered the employee's question "in the moment," you enabled upward delegation. In essence, you have trained your employee not to think on his or her own, but rather to come to you for answers.

As leaders, it is our responsibility to teach those who follow us how to address their own challenges whenever possible.

As an example, I was trained by my early career CEOs to bring in proposed solutions along with any problems or difficulties I might have encountered. Setting this routine expectation in *advance* prepared me to become a more proactive and effective executive. In addition, we saved significant time and resources as we sought expeditious resolutions to problems or as we agreed upon action plans for capitalizing upon our organizational opportunities.

The Root Cause of Upward Delegation

Gracious leaders can empower their teams by asking a few simple, yet critically important, questions. The next time an employee asks you "What should we do?", I encourage you to respond (except in the event of a *legitimate* crisis) by reversing the question. Ask the employee, "What do *you* think we should do?"

In many instances, it is highly likely the employee already knows the answer, and he or she is simply asking your permission to act. If your employees routinely ask you for permission before acting, I challenge you to reflect upon how or why the employees have been conditioned in this manner as opposed to demonstrating their empowerment and independence.

- Is the employee asking permission because he or she is afraid to take a risk?

- Are failures viewed within your organization as negative performances or as learning opportunities?

- Would your employees describe your organizational culture as being punitive? If so, why?

- Is upward delegation simply an ingrained aspect of your corporate culture?

If you find that employees frequently ask permission before acting, you might want to take an introspective look at your own leadership style as well as your organizational culture. Seek to identify the root cause for the team's acting only after receiving *your* permission.

Ask yourself the following questions:

- How does your company purposefully empower its leaders and employees to be proactive in bringing solutions along with problems they report?

- Have any of your leaders been conditioned in other job assignments outside of your organization to delegate upwards as opposed to proposing recommended solutions along with problems that they report? If so, what are you doing to assure they know you expect them to solve their own problems?

- What are your own leadership habits relative to empowering your direct reports to be proactive in bringing solutions along with problems?

- What are you purposefully doing to encourage your direct reports to empower their teams accordingly?

The failure to answer such questions and address the root cause of upward delegation can prevent you, your team members, and your organization-at-large from performing at its peak.

By reversing the question, "What should we do?", and asking employees how they propose to solve the problems, you are showing them you have confidence in their capabilities. You are teaching them to be proactive, independent thinkers.

Some employees try to delegate upwards because they have not yet developed the confidence to propose solutions. Others may fear failure. These employees need to understand that everyone should be expected to learn from their errors. When employees make mistakes, you might consider facilitating a conversation to explore with them the following questions and to make this approach a key ingredient in fostering an empowerment culture that welcomes continuous improvement.

- What did we learn from this situation?

- What went well and what could we have done better?

- Based upon what we learned, how will we approach such problems differently in the future?

Through using this simple approach to a continuous improvement conversation, employees who have previously been chastised for making a mistake can be retrained to understand that mistakes are considered opportunities for ongoing learning and development. Employees can then be groomed to look for the good that occurred and explore how the team can continue to improve.

Learning from errors is important to assure the same mistakes are not repeated and employees overcome the fear of failure while experiencing what true empowerment really means.

Empowering Employees Gives Power to All
Some managers feel needed and gratified by solving problems for their employees as opposed to teaching them to seek problem resolution on their own. Perhaps these managers want to feel like heroes or need to see their fingerprints on the positive outcomes. Or perhaps they think fixing problems offers some semblance of job security because it makes *them* feel indispensable.

While such circumstances might make the managers feel good in the moment, this cycle of dysfunction will deprive employees from developing problem solving skills and mastering the art of taking calculated risks.

Over the years, I have marveled at the frequency with which employees (including leaders) would come to me to complain about a colleague. I have always believed such situations are best solved directly on a peer to peer basis. I have made it my practice to coach my teams to solve such problems on their own.

In considering such situations, I would coach a hypothetical Mary to solve her problem with Jane in the following manner:

Mary, I hear you say that you are having a problem with Jane. As I see it, you have three options.

Option No. 1 is that you can go directly to Jane and resolve your differences.

Option No. 2 is that I will go to Jane and tell her you have a problem with her.

Option No. 3 is that we will go together to Jane and discuss with her the fact you have a problem with her.

Mary, I hope you choose Option No. 1.

As I would point the "Mary's of the world" towards Option No. 1, they invariably voiced discomfort about having the conversations directly with their peers. I coached (and expected) these employees consistently to seek problem resolution independently and directly. In so doing, the Mary's of the world ultimately learned to solve their own problems as opposed to delegating them upwards to me.

As your employees, like Mary, learn to work out their differences directly, not only will they stretch, learn and grow, but they will also become a stronger team of trusted colleagues that can accomplish more together than they had ever previously imagined.

Gracious leaders empower their employees by asking the right questions and teaching them to solve their own problems.

Conversation Starters for Your Team

1. What specific steps will you take to minimize upward delegation and to empower your direct reports to recommend solutions at the same time they bring problems to you?

2. What steps should your organization take to train your employees to offer recommended solutions at the same time they bring problems to the attention of leaders?

3. What specific steps will you take to encourage your employees to act with confidence rather than to ask for your permission to act in situations in which they are fully capable of addressing their concerns?

4. What specific steps will you take to encourage and to support your employees as they learn from their mistakes?

Notes

Place employees in leadership
roles in which they demonstrate
great zeal and where their service
feels second nature to them.

Chapter 10

Gracious Leaders Match Passion with Purpose

E arly in my career at NMMC, our CEO brought in healthcare futurist Leland Kaiser, PhD, to work with our senior team. I remember being so excited about learning from Dr. Kaiser. At the time, he was in such demand that organizations were booking him more than a year in advance.

I was mesmerized by Dr. Kaiser's wisdom, clinging onto every word that he spoke.

Of all the good that he taught us, there was one particular challenge he posed that really struck a chord with me: If we weren't doing what we were created to do, then we could ultimately become physically ill.

Wow! That's heavy stuff!

Not too many months prior to our team's group session with this leading industry expert, I had made the switch from banking into healthcare. I knew I belonged in the healthcare space, and Dr. Kaiser's sage advice further affirmed my conviction to follow my calling to do what I was created to do. My professional passions were clearly matched with the purpose of the work that I would lead.

Matching the Passion of the Person with the Purpose of the Work

It was during this long-anticipated time with Dr. Kaiser that I had an epiphany about my responsibility as a leader to develop those who might follow me throughout my career.

I became committed to matching the *passion of the person with the purpose of the work*. I realized that as a leader, I would need to place employees into leadership roles in which they demonstrated great zeal and where their service would feel like it was second nature to them. A Chinese proverb tells us to "Choose a job you love and you will never have to work a day in your life."

In matching the passion of the person with the purpose of the work, I would henceforth encourage and expect others *to do what they love* and *to do what they were created to do* so that work would be so much more than *just a job*. Through matching the passion of the person with the purpose of the work, I believed that our team would accomplish our work faster, better, and more efficiently and that our employees would be happier and more fulfilled.

Little did I realize at the time the significant impact that matching passion and purpose would have on those with whom I would serve. Aspiring leaders blossomed before my eyes as they rose to the occasion to advance the work of the organization.

Matching Passion with Purpose is Necessary in All Industries

In every industry, leaders are constantly challenged to achieve more with less. Resources are consistently becoming scarcer while expenses seem to increase perpetually. This was certainly the case early on at MCSA, when we faced the significant challenge of transforming our culture as well as our operational and financial performance. There was *so* much work to accomplish.

And even though we received great support from our corporate services team and parent organization, we always seemed to need additional resources to realize our lofty vision.

How could we deliver more with less?

Thank you, Dr. Kaiser. It was at this point that our Leadership Team began to learn the importance of matching the passion of the person with the purpose of the work.

Over time, we determined there were eight different areas of focus in which we needed to accomplish more than our existing resources could support. Some of these areas were obvious early on in our journey, while the need for other areas of emphasis evolved over the course of several years.

The eight areas of focus included Colleague Communications, Colleague Engagement, Community Relations, Growth, Leadership Development, Mission, Patient Experience, and Philanthropy.

Our administrative leadership introduced the concept of Campus Leadership Councils to advance our strategies within these eight areas of opportunity. The leadership councils were formed to allow middle and upper level managers to serve as the "chief executive of sorts" within each of their respective areas of focus.

We recruited our role model leaders and managers to lead these councils as stretch assignments for their professional growth, development and gratification. We were very careful in assuring these leaders were absolutely passionate about the respective area(s) that were assigned to each of them.

We then required all 70-plus leaders to serve on at least one of the eight councils. We further challenged each of these leaders to identify from among the eight councils an area of focus they either were passionate about or an area in which they wanted to learn more.

We told our leaders they could serve on as many of the councils as they desired, but *every* leader had to sign up for at least one of these opportunities to serve in addition to fulfilling their core job responsibilities.

We developed a charter for each council to serve as the True North to guide the work of each group. The charters described the expected goals and deliverables for each council, just as job descriptions define expectations for individual employees.

And then … our C-suite got out of the way.

The council co-chairs and I met monthly so they could share with one another the results their respective councils had achieved. They also shared the aspirations and anticipated challenges they would pursue during the next month.

My role was simple: to ensure we did not drift from our True North. I would ask the co-chairs about any support they needed and inquire what barriers they had encountered that we might help them remove. The co-chairs were leading what they each loved, and it showed through their outstanding results that were accomplished with minimal expense.

As an example, the Colleague Engagement Council (fondly known by some leaders as the Fun Committee) coordinated year-long activities to create a sense of belonging for our employees. From campus picnics to delivering snacks or serving meals at midnight to third shift staff persons, this team loved to help employees know they were appreciated.

The Community Relations Council assured that MCSA was highly visible throughout the greater Westerville area. From coordinating the hospital's role in the Westerville July 4th festivities to recruiting volunteers for the W.A.R.M. (Westerville Area Resource Ministry) Kids' Summer Lunch Program for needy children, this team was passionate about assuring that MCSA was front and center as a community leader.

I am sure Dr. Kaiser would have been proud of these council leaders and their team members. I certainly was overflowing with pride as matching the passion of the person with the purpose of the work became one of our team's key ingredients to catapult our collective performance to new heights.

Gracious leaders unleash the potential of their followers by matching the passion of the person with the purpose of the work.

Conversation Starters for Your Team

1. As the leader of your team, what specific actions will you take to role model your own passion for the work that *you* do?

2. What specific actions will you implement to ensure your employees are passionate about the work they do every day?

3. What actions will you take to encourage your role model employees to volunteer to be involved in work about which they are passionate?

4. What opportunities currently exist for your employees to be engaged in projects in which their professional passions correlate with the purpose of the work?

5. What specific steps will you take to improve your organization's effectiveness in matching the passion of the person with the purpose of the work?

Notes

Believe in the potential of your
followers and provide them
with stretch opportunities
through which their potential
can be realized.

Chapter 11

Gracious Leaders Develop Their People

G racious leaders develop their people by looking for their potential and for believing that the potential of their followers can be realized.

One of my favorite books is *Greater Than Yourself*, by Steven Farber. The premise of the book is that as leaders, we are to identify others whom we want to help become greater than we are. To help others become greater than we are, we should only give these individuals our very best. To give them only our best, *we* must continuously learn and grow.

Once those whom we choose to develop see that we are giving selflessly of ourselves to help them become greater than we are, they will want to follow us and give us their very best at work. In addition, they will strive to recruit other top performers to our team.

Just imagine an organization in which all of its leaders help their followers become greater than they are. Envision that those rising leaders will then cascade the same *Greater Than Yourself* conviction to those whom they mentor.

In this hypothetical situation, I can imagine a positive, viral culture in which the people of the organization are continuously elevating their collective performance. The company's leaders are intentionally, systematically, and continuously developing the organization's most important asset ... its people. Wouldn't you want to work there? I certainly would!

Gracious leaders develop their people by helping them to become greater than themselves. I experienced such selfless leadership from Aubrey Patterson.

The Importance of Stretch Assignments

Mr. Patterson had a knack for placing me in situations I had not previously experienced in the workplace. By his purposeful assignment of stretch projects, he not only exposed me to different organizational functions, but he also role modeled the organization's commitment to accelerate the growth and development of its promising young leaders.

When I was freshly out of the management training program, our vice president of marketing left his position for another role within the organization. Even though I had no experience in marketing, Mr. Patterson appointed me to serve as the interim vice president of marketing for this regional financial services organization. I instantly found myself in a significant role overseeing a small staff, including one employee who was more than twice my age. This responsibility appeared daunting at the time.

Through this experience, Mr. Patterson provided me the opportunity to be in the board room at a very early stage of my career. And I learned more about marketing in a short span of time than I ever could have learned from a textbook.

During my tenure with Bank of Mississippi, Mr. Patterson assigned a variety of special team projects to another young banker and me. I remember thinking on multiple occasions, "I don't know how to do this, but we'll figure it out!"

One example was when Mr. Patterson handed us two boxes of contemporary financial planning software, and he assigned us the task of developing the budgets for our community banks. Little did I know at the time that I would be living with budgets for the rest of my professional life. What a great experience that was for a neophyte banker!

Mr. Patterson also assigned to our team the responsibility of developing the plans and measurement processes to implement a personal banker program within our banking system. And Mr. Patterson assigned each of us the opportunity to assist with the management oversight of nine community banks.

Not only did these endeavors provide value to the bank, but they also taught me increasing confidence to accept new and exciting challenges that helped me grow as a young professional.

Whether it was internal stretch assignments or external opportunities—such as serving on the board of the Mississippi Economic Council, the executive committee of the Community Development Foundation, or the president of the Tupelo Chapter of the American Institute of Banking—I was placed in those leadership roles because Aubrey Patterson believed in my potential, and he gave me opportunities to see that potential realized. Mr. Patterson purposefully advocated for my professional growth and development, and he continued to do so … *even* after I left the bank for the healthcare industry.

Mr. Patterson, my first and favorite professional mentor, taught me important lessons that are applicable at work and in life at large. He taught me *how to become comfortable being uncomfortable.*

Mr. Patterson taught me that my professional journey will always include lifelong learning. And he taught me the importance of seeing the potential in others, in believing the potential of others can be realized, in fostering that potential, and in giving those individuals opportunities to be successful by challenging them to play at the top of their game. For all of the leadership lessons that Mr. Patterson has role modeled for me, I shall be forever grateful.

I am just one person of many who has had the good fortune and, indeed, the blessing of working for Aubrey Patterson. His leadership has made a profound difference in the lives of all who have followed him. His extraordinary, positive impact will no doubt be felt for many generations to come.

In following Mr. Patterson's footsteps as my role model for Gracious Leadership, I have sought throughout my career to identify others who have the potential to become great leaders.

It has been my mission and my professional destiny to help them become all that they were created to be … indeed to become greater than I am.

Helping Others Become Comfortable Being Uncomfortable
Throughout my career, I have sought to emulate Mr. Patterson's practice of developing those whom I have had the joy of leading by helping them become comfortable being uncomfortable.

Several employees come to my mind. One, a shy word-processing clerk from the bank, ultimately became a confident leader within a health system foundation. Another, the line director of a clinical department, assumed the stretch assignment of serving as the administrative liaison for a multi-million-dollar construction project. And a sales director with excellent project management skills took on the high profile stretch assignment of coordinating logistics associated with the expansion of a significant clinical product line.

In each of these examples, I was purposeful in giving these individuals the opportunity to lead outside of their traditional job functions ... to become comfortable being uncomfortable so they might be better positioned for future promotions with broader job responsibilities.

While working for one the four healthcare systems in which I have served, I identified a bright, young professional whose work product was among the best that I had ever seen. After my being recruited to a new health system for a broader C-suite opportunity, one of the first steps I took was to recruit this rising star to my new organization. Shortly after this individual accepted the role and relocated to serve as my direct report, I was asked to assume an advancement within the organization. Knowing the vast potential of this talented young executive, I asked this person to serve as my interim successor. The individual served with goodness and with grace. I am very pleased to share that several years after the interim assignment had been completed, this individual was named to serve in the same C-Suite role on a permanent basis.

Helping the next generation of leaders become comfortable being uncomfortable as they stretch, learn, and grow may well be one of the most important responsibilities that gracious leaders will ever accomplish.

The Joy of Seeing Potential Realized
While I have many fond memories of mentoring those whom I have had the pleasure of leading, I treasure a particular memory about one of my favorite mentees.

Our Leadership Development Council had taken flight and was providing outstanding professional development opportunities for our team of 70-plus leaders. In addition to growth and development, we sought to showcase examples of great leadership and innovation within the campus.

In the spirit of doing more with less, we were placing an emphasis on managing labor costs. I had asked this mentee, a nurse manager, to share with the entire Leadership Team the approach she had taken to manage overtime in a manner that also fostered positive employee engagement.

During the next leadership development retreat, the nurse manager delivered the presentation as I had requested. The leaders listened with great interest, and then we moved on to the remaining activities of the day.

Several days later, the nurse manager asked to meet with me. She shared that she needed to let me know she felt uncomfortable giving the presentation during the retreat.

I thanked her for voicing her concern, and then I asked her the following question:

"What did you see from the front of the room as you were making the presentation?"

She said, "I saw my peers, and it made me uncomfortable. After all, what right do I have to tell others how to lead their departments?"

I shared with her that her work was excellent and, as an organization committed to continuous learning and improvement, we as leaders needed to share best practices. I then said the following to her.

"From the front of the room, you saw your peers, and it made you feel uncomfortable. Let me tell you what I saw from the back of the room. I saw a future Chief Nursing Officer."

Her eyes grew wide. She smiled gently, and she quietly said, "Oh, I see."

Then I talked further with her about an important lesson of responsibility I had learned from Mr. Patterson ... that as a leader, it is my role to look for potential in others, and to develop those individuals by helping them learn to become comfortable being uncomfortable. That's how we can become all that we were created to be.

By the way, that nurse manager is "oh so close" to becoming a Chief Nursing Officer. I rather suspect that one of these days she may become a hospital president.

Gracious leaders develop their people by looking for and believing in their potential. In so doing, we fulfill our leadership destiny by helping others become all that they were created to be ... indeed, to become greater than we are.

Conversation Starters for Your Team

1. What success stories can you currently celebrate regarding the internal growth and development of your employees?

2. What specific steps will you take to be more purposeful in identifying high potential employees who can be developed for stretch assignments or expanded roles?

3. What specific steps will you take to be more purposeful in making significant stretch assignments to develop your employees while also delivering incremental value to your organization?

4. What specific steps will you take to facilitate your employees' ability to be comfortable being uncomfortable as they stretch, learn, and grow?

Notes

Accountability should constitute
the assurance *and* the celebration
of achieving the right results.

Chapter 12

Gracious Leaders Require Accountability

G racious leaders are not *soft* leaders. Much to be contrary, gracious leaders *require* accountability for results from themselves and from their teams.

I have long been a proponent of Triple-A Leadership as critical "must haves" for sustainable organizational success. My definition of Triple-A Leadership includes accountability, alignment, and acknowledgement.

- **Accountability** starts and stops with the leader. One of the kindest and most important things a leader can do is to be crystal clear with employees about expectations. Employees can only be held accountable for achieving the right results when they definitively know what is expected of them. Failure by leaders to define goals clearly is like asking a blindfolded person to hit a target.

- **Alignment** means that the work of employees must correlate with the organization's purpose. Employees need a clear line of sight between what they do every day and how their efforts contribute to the organization's success. When the team's actions are aligned with organizational goals, the probability of success can increase dramatically.

- With **Acknowledgement**, employees need and deserve feedback in a predictable manner. They want to know how they're doing in supporting organizational success. We'll talk more about acknowledgement (feedback and recognition) in chapters 15 and 17.

While accountability, alignment, and acknowledgement are all key strategies for gracious leaders to employ as they guide their teams to optimal outcomes, this chapter will focus on accountability, as it is by far one of the most important ingredients for getting to peak performance and sustainable success.

Accountability is Not a Four-Letter Word

Throughout the years, I have found some people bristle when they hear the word accountability. It's as though they think it is a four-letter word. When implemented with grace, however, nothing could be further from the truth. It is absolutely possible to have an accountable culture that is also compassionate. The two approaches do not have to be mutually exclusive.

For the gracious leader, accountability should constitute the assurance *and* the celebration of achieving the *right results*.

Accountability for Self as Leader

When I worked for Dan Wilford, I learned a lot about accountability for self and for the team.

Shortly after I went to work for NMMC, Mr. Wilford told me during a one-on-one meeting that I should not try to keep up with his pace. At the time, I didn't know what that really meant, but it didn't take long to figure it out.

Mr. Wilford was nothing short of amazing. The man had a remarkable work ethic. Clearly, he loved hospital administration. He also demonstrated tireless zeal and dedication, as he was doing what he was created to do.

His typical work day started with a six-mile run prior to his arrival at the hospital long before 7 a.m. He worked non-stop until the evening, went home to spend time with his family, and then reportedly worked a few more hours until he retired for the night.

Mr. Wilford was involved as a leader in a variety of important community and religious organizations. In his spare time on weekends in the fall, he was a Southwestern Conference football official. He later became an NFL football official.

One of the many lessons I learned from Dan Wilford was never to expect more from my staff than I expected of myself. This was an important lesson I have carried forth throughout my leadership journey.

Accountability for Confidence and Humility
In being accountable for yourself, gracious leaders should look in the mirror continuously and seek to see what those who follow you will see. They have the confidence to lead boldly with courage. They also have the humility to say, "I don't know," "I made a mistake," "I am sorry," or "I need your help."

I shared with you in Chapter 1 that when I had announced my intention to work for North Mississippi Medical Center, the bank's Chairman of the Board and CEO called me to his office and told me that I was making a mistake by leaving his organization. Several years later, this same executive became the Chairman of the Board of NMMC. Immediately prior to a particular meeting at the hospital, the bank's CEO and I coincidentally had some time alone to converse.

During this discussion, out of the blue, the CEO reminded me that as I was contemplating a move into healthcare he had cautioned me that I was making a mistake. A powerful corporate executive, as well as a sage and confident community leader, this CEO role modeled humility by telling me *he* was the one who had made the mistake. He shared his belief and affirmation I had made the *right* professional decision, as healthcare was exactly where I belonged!

Humility in a leader is a not a sign of weakness, but rather of strength, wisdom and, courage. Strength is required when a leader needs to admit his or her decision prevented the team from achieving the right results. Wisdom is demonstrated when leaders acknowledge they don't have all of the answers. And courage is in order, as an example, when a leader in the presence of peers asks a question for explanation or clarification, knowing others in the room invariably want to know the same information, but will not speak up due to a fear of appearing uninformed.

Through being completely human, gracious leaders are secure enough to know they can be vulnerable with their teams and with others. And teams want to follow a leader who is real, confident, and humble.

Accountability of the Team
Gracious leaders are accountable for themselves, and they expect accountability from their teams.

One leadership lesson I learned from Mr. Wilford was an excellent process to keep team accountability in the forefront of leaders' minds. He required his directors and those above them to complete a quarterly report through which the leaders would share the status of goal progress.

Over the years, I have adapted this report to track the results important to my teams' performance at the time.

I have used this accountability report as an opportunity for leaders to showcase the great results their teams have accomplished and to assure they consistently lead their teams to pursue the right *outcomes.*

The report was simple, yet highly impactful. To follow are the topics that each leader had to address on a systematic basis:

- What was the most significant accomplishment your team achieved during the past month that you want to celebrate?

- What is your team's most significant challenge you anticipate for next month *and* that you need someone else's assistance to address?

- What are your current results on our balanced scorecard?

  o In areas where variances to plan exist, explain the actions you are taking to achieve the right results.

  o Report only on *actual outcomes* as opposed to *activities* that were employed to achieve the required results.

- Share a story about an employee who went above and beyond the call of duty for a patient, a guest, a co-worker, or the community.

In addition to submitting this report on a systematic basis, I have had my leaders participate in monthly accountability meetings with their peers. Not only did the group meetings conserve time, but they also helped reinforce accountability for results because the discussions were held in the presence of their co-workers.

We used every possible effort to assure a positive tone in these meetings. We openly praised the achievement of the right results, and we inquired as to what barriers we could remove to help these leaders achieve peak performance.

Make no mistake about it. Every leader in attendance fully understood that these meetings were about our intent not only *to inspire* but also to *require* accountability for the right results. Any performance deficiencies were discussed in a private setting.

Accountability meetings with a positive focus can be very important in creating a culture of compassionate accountability. You also can achieve high-performance accountability in a gracious manner with your team. Just adapt the report to track the most important results to your organization. And remember to bookend accountability with praise, to counsel with grace, and to avoid confusing activities with outcomes.

Compassionate Accountability Can Reap Great Rewards

I hope you will discover your team's results can be remarkable, just as I have had the pleasure of celebrating the great outcomes of teams I have led. As for Dan Wilford, I believe his leadership expertise related to accountability has had a long-lasting imprint on those who served with him. Years after Mr. Wilford left North Mississippi Medical Center, NMMC and its parent organization, North Mississippi Health Services, became the first two-time healthcare Malcolm Baldridge Award recipient in the program's 25-year history.

The Malcolm Baldridge National Quality Award is the only formal recognition of performance excellence of public and private United States organizations given by the President of the United States. NMMC first won this prestigious award in 2006, and after deploying the Baldridge Criteria to its entire healthcare system, NMHS won the award in 2012.

Mr. Wilford clearly set the bar high for how to run a peak performance hospital and healthcare system. I am confident other leaders who have followed him have joined me in building upon his conviction of achieving compassionate accountability and consistent excellence with grace.

The Need for Thick Skin

As you become committed to building a more accountable culture, you will likely need to introduce more specificity into your team goals so your staff understands exactly what they are expected to accomplish. This is critically important.

While many of your employees will likely welcome this clear expression of expectations, some employees may resist the clarity. Frankly, it is these employees who may not want to be held accountable for achieving anything that is specific.

You'll need to have thick skin if you hear from a vocal minority that "You're micromanaging us. What you're doing by using measurable goals is counter to our culture. You don't trust us if you think we need measurable goals."

On multiple occasions throughout my career, I have encountered resistance from some staff members when clear and measurable, specific goals were initially introduced. In addition to the above excuses, some employees would argue, "There is no way we can possibly accomplish those results within such tight time lines."

I recall vividly a time in which our organization had launched a new strategic plan. We had introduced an accountability process through which clearly articulated, short-term and long-term goals had been created. Diverse teams that were working in parallel were assigned the responsibility to accomplish specific results within definitive timelines.

While the short-term timelines were aggressive, the ability to achieve the desired results was clearly within reach. And the opportunity to harvest some quick wins was vitally important in building momentum and enthusiasm for the implementation of this new plan.

An executive who had been designated as a champion for one of the strategies told me emphatically there was no way the short-term results could be achieved within the targeted timeline. I shared with this leader that the results were in fact possible and we really needed him to give the process a chance. He was not happy.

To make a long story short, amazing results were accomplished and celebrated, and this executive ultimately became an advocate and cheerleader for using this approach for the systematic implementation of strategy.

As employees embrace goal clarity, they can begin to soar. Others who are clearly not excited about this shift in organizational conviction and accountability may continue to voice opposition. As a result, you may find yourself in a situation where you may lose a few managers and employees along the way if they are not willing to buy into this necessary culture change.

Although it can be painful early on, the results your team can achieve will be well worth the journey. Just know this: Culture change is hard when accountability has been missing.

As a gracious leader who expects increasing accountability for excellence, it is important to stay the course, not take criticisms personally, and work in tandem with your HR business partners. Together, you should be able to traverse any rocky waters you may encounter.

On your journey towards compassionate accountability, also remember that the kindest thing a gracious leader can ever do for employees is to be crystal clear about expectations. Goal clarity and role clarity are "must have" building blocks for organizational accountability, peak performance, and sustained success.

Conversation Starters for Your Team

1. What specific steps will you take to ensure you are being crystal clear with your employees regarding what you expect from them?

2. What opportunities for improvement exist within your organization to ensure all employees clearly understand what is expected of them?

3. What specific actions will you take to ensure your employees have a clear line of sight between what they do every day and your organization's mission and goals?

4. What specific actions should your organization take to ensure all of your employees have a clear line of sight between what they do every day and your organization's mission and goals?

5. What accountability processes will you implement to assure and to celebrate the achievement of the right outcomes from your employees?

Ask for opportunity where merited for yourself or others; confront bully behavior when needed; and always do what's right, even when it's not popular.

Chapter 13

Gracious Leaders are Courageous

G racious leaders must demonstrate courage in a wide variety of circumstances. They may find themselves in a position to take a stand for their own well-being or advancement. They clearly must demonstrate courage as they advocate on behalf of others. In all cases, gracious leaders must always do what's right, they must do what's fair, and they must be consistent.

The Courage to Ask for Opportunity

In Chapter 4, I shared that when I was being recruited to Ohio I asked for a commitment that I would be given the opportunity to lead one of the MCHS hospitals as openings became available.

Had I not had the courage to ask for this specific opportunity, I am certain I never would have led a hospital. And I would have missed out on the joy I received through serving with the people of the MCSA campus.

At one point in my career, I was serving as a director for a medical center. After several promotions had been made to co-workers, I decided to ask my boss to change my title to reflect more accurately the magnitude of work I was leading.

When I garnered the courage to make the ask, my boss inquired as to why it was important to me to have my title changed.

Without hesitation, I respectfully replied, "Let me answer your question with a question. When you were recruited here, why was it important to you that your title be changed from administrator to president? Was it to reflect more appropriately the scope of work that you would be leading?"

He was quiet while I was absolutely *dying inside*! The silence seemed to last a lifetime.

And then he said, "You raise a good point."

Within a few weeks, he announced my promotion to vice president. And over the next few years, this executive continued to expand my responsibilities to include three additional departments *without* my having to ask!

I hasten to tell you this story is *not* important merely because I was successful in receiving a title change. Rather, if I had not found the courage to ask for what I thought was appropriate at that time, I might have held back in other circumstances later on in my professional life in which courage was required and the stakes were high.

As such, I am always purposeful in encouraging others to find the courage to *ask for opportunity*. Not only can the results include promotions, but they also can include stretch assignments that are critically important in paving the way for new or expanded roles.

Just remember, first things do come first. Your prospects of getting the promotion you want or new job you've dreamed about will more likely happen when you are a trusted, proven performer.

My point, however, is that just because you are a trusted, proven performer does not mean that you'll get what you want and deserve.

Sometimes you just have to ask!

The Courage to Ask on Behalf of Others

From time to time, it will be important for leaders to advocate on behalf of others, particularly when the other person isn't comfortable making the ask.

I'll never forget the time when our CEO decided to start a new standing meeting every week at 7 a.m. Within healthcare, it's common to have meetings that start as early as 5:30 a.m., and other meetings that end well after 9 p.m. That's the nature of the business, as you meet with physicians when they are available, either before or after their patient care hours.

For this particular meeting, none of the participants were physicians.

I learned one of my co-workers, a highly respected professional who was a single parent, had no one to take care of her elementary-aged child before the school's official start time. As a result, she was actually leaving the child unattended outside the doors of the school.

I approached the CEO and respectfully asked if there was a particular reason why this new standing meeting needed to be held at 7 a.m. He said, "No particular reason." I shared the story with him, and he changed the meeting time immediately, with no hesitation.

Asking on behalf of others is what gracious leaders do. The higher you rise within an organization, as a gracious and giving leader you will spend more and more of your time advocating and acting on behalf of those who follow you.

Whether you are asking for a raise for a rising star who is taking on material stretch assignments or if you're asking the right questions to assure that pay equity is achieved, gracious leaders ask on behalf of others simply because it's the right thing to do.

The Courage to Confront a Bully

I can already sense your panic, as confronting a bully is rarely at the top of the list of our favorite things to do. Yet confronting bullies is one of the most important things that a gracious leader may ever have to do.

There's an old saying, "If you permit it, you promote it." Remaining silent with bullies is nothing short of an endorsement of bad behavior.

I recall a meeting I was having with a high-ranking executive. We were discussing several topics, and one of the topics clearly struck a nerve with this individual.

The executive exploded ... not for something that I had done, but because the individual was incredibly angry about the situation we were discussing. The executive ranted and raved on and on, and then ultimately calmed down and apologized for the outburst.

I was shocked and totally caught off guard by this tirade. I told the executive not to worry about it, and I would speak up in the future if I felt that a line had been crossed.

Then, at the end of the day, I went home and was furious with myself over the weekend for not calling out this inappropriate behavior in the moment.

Through permitting it, I had promoted bad behavior unbecoming for a leader. To make matters worse, I had verbalized an acceptance of this unacceptable tirade by inferring a line had not already been crossed.

The following week, I asked to meet again with the executive. I told the individual that during our earlier meeting, I had committed to speak up if a line of unacceptable behavior had been crossed. I further shared that the line had indeed been crossed when rage was directed at me.

I committed I would happily be available if this executive needed to vent in a controlled manner, but I would never, ever again tolerate this type of outburst.

And it never happened again ... at least not with me.

Confronting a Bully Boss

During the Q&A session following a presentation I made regarding Gracious Leadership, an attendee asked me how he should handle a bully boss. I shared with the individual my thoughts as to what to do in such a situation.

First, it is necessary to assess your personal values and professional principles and decide if tolerating such behavior is compromising what is important to you.

Throughout this book, you have learned that fundamental respect is a critical "must have" in our personal and professional relationships. As a result, for me, doing nothing with a bully boss would *not* be an option.

I personally would go directly to the individual at the right time. With kind candor, I would describe how the behaviors were adversely affecting the team, including me. I would share with the individual that I am incredibly loyal and I consider it to be my responsibility to tell my boss what he or she needs to hear, even if it may not be what the individual wants to hear. I would then ask the individual how I could help.

And I would end by thanking my boss that we have a solid relationship of trust in which we can be transparent with one another.

When confronting a bully boss, one of two possible responses might be anticipated. The boss may be shocked to receive this feedback and demonstrate remorse that he or she has grown comfortable demonstrating such untenable behavior. Sometimes individuals who are bullies don't realize how their behaviors affect others. In such situations, there may be an opportunity for change if the individual has any emotional intelligence *and* is willing to work on the necessary change. That being said, it is very hard work to break old habits and, when under pressure, people tend to regress to the old way of life.

The other potential reply might be complete denial and anger with an "I'm the boss and I don't care" attitude. "That's just the way I am." This hypothetical boss might "shoot the messenger" through retaliation and continue the same pattern of bad behavior. If there's no change in the bully's behavior, or if retaliation occurred, I personally would not stay. It's time for Plan B.

In reality, many people will, unfortunately, not confront a bully boss. Of course, they need the steady income to provide for their families, and they may rightfully fear retribution and potentially the loss of a job. The issue of confronting a bully can be very tough, but in reality, it comes down to what's important to you.

Only you can determine if you can experience sustainable happiness in a toxic work environment. And you are the only person who can assess what impact that toxicity might have on your interactions with your family and others when you leave the office. After all, our families need and deserve us to bring home our best at the end of the day.

Just remember that the tone of an organization is clearly set at the top, and how leaders behave will cast long shadows, not only throughout their businesses, but also into our homes.

The Courage to be Truthful and to Do What's Right ... Always

My conviction to tell the truth without compromise and do what's right came from my father. He put a lot on the line when he, in Mississippi, advocated equal rights for all people at a point in history when equality was not popular.

In 1964, as the attorney for the Leake County School Board, my father guided the board members to follow the federal mandate for the schools to be integrated. Our school district was among the first in Mississippi to comply with this highly controversial law. My father was one of the individuals who escorted African-American first grader Debra Lewis safely to her desk on her first day at Carthage Elementary School.

My father had the courage to stand firm in his convictions to do what was right, even as our community was split wide apart over desegregation. As a result of his conviction to do the right thing, our family endured significant duress as my father became an enemy target of the Ku Klux Klan.

To put this into perspective, our family lived only 25 miles from Philadelphia, Mississippi, where three Civil Rights workers were slain. My father had to meet periodically with the FBI, and he had to carry a gun for his own protection (and that of our family).

My father was a role model of honesty, integrity, and courage, and I am grateful that my brother and I had the blessing of being raised by parents who lived their convictions and values without regard to the cost.

Our father taught us to be uncompromisingly honest and do what is right, to do what is fair, and to be consistent ... always.

Within the workplace, it doesn't matter if you're addressing human resources issues, if you're deciding who works on a holiday weekend, or if you're casting a tiebreaker vote on a tough decision. It doesn't matter if you are asked to accommodate a favor or make an exception to an important organizational rule.

When you always do what's right and fair, and you are always consistent, your staff and other key stakeholders will know that they can trust you when the stakes are high.

Gracious leaders are courageous. They ask for opportunities when merited for themselves or for others, they confront bully behavior when needed, and they always do what's right, even and especially when it's not popular.

Conversation Starters for Your Team

1. What steps will you take to encourage your employees to have the courage to ask for stretch assignments or expanded opportunities?

2. Describe several examples of ways through which you have advocated on behalf of your team members. What steps will you take to be more effective in advocating on behalf of your employees?

3. Think about several examples of how you have done what was right and what was fair and that you were consistent when the stakes were high. What steps will you take to address any opportunities for improvement?

4. What actions will you take to ensure you *and* your leaders always do what is right, what is fair, and that you are consistent?

5. Think about any examples of how you have promoted bully behaviors by remaining silent. What specific steps will you take to ensure bully behaviors are appropriately addressed?

6. What opportunities for improvement exist in which you need to be courageous in asking on your own behalf as well as on behalf of others? What specific steps will you take to address these opportunities for improvement?

Notes

Seek feedback for your own
professional development *and*
to improve organizational
performance.

Chapter 14

Gracious Leaders Seek Feedback

G racious leaders seek feedback because they understand continuous improvement is not solely about business processes. It is also about seeking input for our own professional growth and development.

The request for feedback should be sincerely expressed, and, in a perfect world, a response of gratitude should be offered whenever much needed input is received. Whenever a leader expresses appreciation for feedback, the door opens wider for value-added insights to flow. Conversely, when an individual is defensive in receiving constructive input, the odds of receiving well-intended feedback in the future may be greatly diminished.

Being grateful for feedback is not necessarily easy to accomplish. Feedback can be difficult to hear, even when it's shared with grace. And feedback can be counterproductive if conveyed in a spiteful or ungracious manner.

Much Needed Feedback Can Be Difficult to Receive
Many years ago, I received feedback I did not request but needed more

than I realized at the time: I was not a good listener. Frankly, I had a blind spot regarding this important leadership skill.

The feedback was shared with hurtful words. I remember shedding many tears in private for several days because the words cut deeply. Was hurtful feedback necessary to help me become a better listener? I personally don't think so. But those were the cards I was dealt. And it was up to me to figure out how to play them.

After sifting through the painful words to get to the core of the feedback, I decided to take the input to heart and to focus on what mattered most from the comments about listening. In so doing, I began my journey to become a more purposeful and diligent listener.

Ultimately, I realized the feedback was indeed a gift, and I became grateful for the motivation to improve my listening skills. In fact, listening became one of the most important aspects of my leadership platform. Without receiving this kick in the pants to become a better listener, my career could easily have been derailed.

Many years have passed since I received that necessary feedback. The pain of that experience has waned. And years later, I reached out to the individual who shared with me that much needed, but hard to hear, feedback.

I expressed to her my gratitude for her role in conveying those insights because she helped to make me a better listener and, as a result, a better leader.

Seeking Feedback for Your Own Continuous Improvement
As a part of my lifelong learning journey, I have appreciated the opportunity to work with some extraordinary executive coaches. From 360-degree appraisals to directly asking my mentors, peers, and followers for their feedback regarding how I might be a better leader, I have been proactive in seeking input from others for my own continuous improvement.

As an example, I have made it my practice to periodically ask my direct reports, key customers, and partners to share with me one specific aspect about *how* I lead that I should *change* so I might become a more effective leader.

Without exception, those to whom I have posed this question have been appreciative of the opportunity to offer their insights and felt valued that I was genuinely interested in their opinions.

If you have an opportunity for improvement in any of your leadership competencies, you might consider asking a mentor, peer, or trusted direct report to serve as your accountability partner. Share with this person your game plan for improvement and ask that individual for feedback on your self-improvement plan. Then routinely ask and rely upon that individual to provide you with ongoing feedback and candor when improvements are realized, as well as constructive input when any regression might be observed.

Asking such questions and engaging trusted confidants can help you in addressing your own blind spots. Seeking such feedback can also demonstrate to your key stakeholders that you are a role model for continuous self-improvement, as you are committed to being the very best leader possible.

Those individuals who have been courageous and forthright with me about my own opportunities for improvement have been my trusted advisors whom I knew would act in my best interest and especially in the best interest of the organization. It was also these same leaders whose growth and development I have strived to support in a purposeful manner so they could become all they were created to be.

Seeking Feedback for Organizational Performance

In Chapter 7, we discussed the need for gracious leaders to listen with purpose and respond with care. Within that chapter, I introduced the concept of Three Powerful Questions:

- What one thing should we do to make our customer's experience better?

- What one thing should we change to make your work life better?

- Is there anything else you'd like to discuss?

These Three Powerful Questions can produce profound insights as you seek feedback from internal or external stakeholders regarding ways through which your organization can improve its performance. Through using these simple, open-ended questions, other individuals are given blank slates to share any hot topics or burning platforms.

As an example, in seeking feedback from customers, I have held Industrial Round Table discussions during which our C-Suite executives would meet with small groups of the chief executive officers and chief human resource officers of the region's largest self-funded employers. The agenda was not to ask our guests to tell us how well we were doing in meeting the needs of their companies, but rather to seek their feedback on how we could *better* meet their needs.

We specifically asked these corporate executives one of the Three Powerful Questions ... "What one thing should we do to make our customers' experience better?" To cut to the chase, *we wanted our customers to tell us what was broken.*

A prevailing theme arose in these feedback sessions, during which, not surprisingly, the employers complained about their companies' ever-increasing healthcare costs. Within this healthcare system, direct contracting with self-funded companies was becoming an important market strategy. Because of the employers' feedback, our healthcare system adopted a "Zero Price Increase Policy" for a few years. By using this customer feedback and by following through with an associated, direct and high impact response, our healthcare system improved brand loyalty and grew our commercial market share.

On one occasion, when I was new to the organization, I was seeking internal stakeholder feedback regarding ways through which we might improve organizational performance. During a series of town hall meetings, I specifically asked another one of the Three Powerful Questions. I encouraged employees to share openly their answers to the query, "What one thing we should change to make your work life better?"

The most prominent theme was that the employees wanted leadership to get rid of the "bad apples" and to ensure every employee was carrying a fair share of the load. The insights of these employees proved to be accurate, and our leadership followed through by implementing processes in which accountability expectations would prospectively be clearly stated and consistently applied.

From my experience, seeking feedback for improving organizational performance is not only an easy thing to do, but it is also strategically eye-opening as the internal and external stakeholders have been ready, willing, and able to share their rich insights.

From 'Round the Clock' meetings with employees to early morning and late evening meetings with physicians ... from skip level meetings with middle managers to smaller round table discussions with key stakeholders, gracious leaders can choose from a wide variety of venues through which to obtain valuable feedback that can foster organizational optimization.

Gracious leaders seek feedback routinely and strive to honor that feedback whenever possible as they lead their teams on the journey of continuous improvement. The key ingredients are to be proactive, genuine, and uncompromisingly sincere. In so doing, the people who know you and your organization the best can be comfortable in offering honest and constructive insights that can support your team's journey to peak performance.

Conversation Starters for Your Team

1. What specific steps will you take to improve your effectiveness in seeking feedback from others for your ongoing professional development?

2. What specific steps will you take to seek feedback from others to affect improvements within your direct area of responsibility, as well as within the organization at large?

3. What specific processes will you implement to ensure you are *systematically* seeking feedback for your ongoing professional development?

4. What specific processes will you implement to ensure you are *systematically* seeking feedback for improvements within your direct area of responsibility, as well as within the organization at large?

5. Ask your direct reports to share with you one thing that you should do differently to be more effective in leading your team. Explore any themes that exist from the feedback you receive. What specific steps will you take to honor this feedback and to share with your team what you are going to do differently as a result of their feedback to improve your effectiveness as a leader?

Employees crave feedback
to know they are making a
difference.

Chapter 15

Gracious Leaders Provide Feedback

I once worked with a leader who held the philosophy that you have to tear down people before you can build them up. Rest assured, you will not find advocacy for that philosophy anywhere within this book! In fact, it is difficult for me to fathom why any leader would have a desire to perpetuate such a counterproductive conviction.

Gracious leaders must be *people builders, not people breakers.* When gracious leaders provide feedback, it is a *gift.* The feedback should be clear and constructive. It should be "in the moment" whenever possible. And feedback should be specific and sincere.

As a high school and college athlete, I well remember the impact of feedback from my coach and the fans. When I was in eighth grade, I had worked very hard to improve my technique in shooting jump shots. One day at the end of practice, I was the last athlete to leave the court. I took the opportunity to shoot just one more basket. Coach Joe Edd Kea happened to be in the gym, and he said, "Smith, that jump shot looks pretty good."

Those few words of encouragement were all I needed to be inspired to work even harder ... to strive to shoot a better jump shot and be a better athlete. In fact, if Coach Kea had told me to jump off of a bridge, I would likely have said, "Yes, sir! Which side?"

Accolades for Expectations

Let's take the sports analogies one step further. Imagine you're attending your favorite team's college football game. It's a beautiful fall afternoon, and your team is ranked high in the national polls. Although your team is playing a fierce and competitive rival, your team is *expected* to win the game.

The stadium is packed with spectators. Kickoff takes place, and your team quickly advances down the field and scores.

And ... no one cheers.

In fact, no one cheers for a great sack, a 100-yard kickoff return, an interception, or any other subsequent great play or score. Even the coach provides no feedback during the game.

Why was no one cheering? Because your team was *expected* to win, and based upon the philosophy that feedback is not warranted when expectations are met, the team neither needed nor deserved any feedback.

Now how ridiculous is that?

Yet every day in organizations throughout Corporate America, some leaders believe their employees and teams don't need feedback on a job well-done because everyone is *expected* to do good work.

I was recently asked to consult with a company within the financial services industry. As part of the engagement, I interviewed leaders and managers from throughout the organization. Several of the retail managers expressed frustration that their employees had made an impressive number of referrals to specialty departments, but they received no feedback.

Expressions of gratitude were perceived as unnecessary because referrals were *expected* as part of the employees' goals. As a result, some of the retail managers and employees had adopted the feeling, "Why bother to send any more referrals? No one recognizes our efforts. No one seems to care."

Such a situation represents not only a missed opportunity for the organization, but also an absolute travesty. The omission of feedback for referrals was not intentional. Yet the absence of feedback had the potential to diminish the future profitability of this organization as important, high-yield referrals were on the road to rapid erosion.

Employees Crave Feedback

I have found over the years that employees crave feedback to understand how they're doing. In fact, they are starving for affirmation from their leaders so they know they are making a positive difference.

In an era in which leaders must consistently achieve more with less, "Thank you," "Great job," or "I appreciate your fine work" do not constitute extra line items within the budget. Providing affirmation and constructive feedback do not require any incremental monetary investment. They do, however, require leaders to be *purposeful* and *sincere* in committing to the establishment of predictable feedback processes.

Well-designed feedback methodologies lead to the systematic recognition of the great work the organization wants and needs to replicate. And purposeful feedback leads to performance improvement when deficiencies exist. In either circumstance, employees want and deserve to know how they are performing.

Feedback Should be Continuous

In a perfect world, feedback should be continuous and "in the moment" as opposed to being reserved for the formal performance appraisal or periodic staff meetings. Can you imagine a football coach who provides feedback to the players only when the game is officially over? That coach isn't likely to make it through one season!

Different schools of thought exist as to whether performance evaluations add value. I have been amazed at the number of leaders and managers who view the performance evaluation process as a nuisance requirement from HR. These individuals go through the motions so they can stay off HR's naughty list. Frankly, they are doing a disservice to their employees and the organization at large.

Labor costs rank very high among organizational expenses across many industries. Failure to take seriously the performance evaluation process leads to subpar productivity and suboptimal organizational performance. In short, leaders who view the performance management process as a rote exercise in futility can cost their respective organizations millions of dollars in lost opportunity.

Managing Performance as Accountability is Increased

Throughout my career, I have taken seriously the importance of providing feedback to employees through properly conducted performance evaluations and performance conversations.

In Chapter 12—regarding accountability—I shared the importance for leaders to express clear expectations to employees and then to hold the employees accountable for meeting those expectations.

In one organization, as we raised the bar of accountability we noticed a steady flow of managers going to HR with the message that "We need to fire John. He's not meeting expectations." The HR leader pulled the employee's file only to find out that John's last few performance evaluations all indicated his work was satisfactory *based upon the manager's annual review of his performance.* There was no documentation to the contrary.

Same song, second verse for Mary, Joe, and Sally ... and on and on. No evidence existed to substantiate that many employees had ever been told they were missing the mark on performance. In fact, we found in several situations the root cause of poor performance was that the manager had not been crystal clear in expressing expectations to the employees. Remember, accountability starts and stops with the leader.

As a result, we retrained our managers on how to coach and counsel employees *first to understand* and *then to meet* expectations, working closely with HR to assure we were being fair and consistent. Then we followed by retraining our managers on the importance of both the annual performance evaluation and the one-on-one performance conversation.

In the beginning, we encountered some resistance, particularly from those managers who had large spans of control. Performance evaluations can require a lot of time when they are done correctly. And then you add the actual time required to conduct one-on-one performance conversations. That sounds like a lot to expect from your managers.

But we *did* expect this level of commitment from managers because employees were our most valuable asset. We needed everyone to play at the top of their game to reach peak performance. You should do the same. In fact, organizations would be well-served to incorporate performance feedback training as an important component of any manager or leader annual training curriculum. Alternatively, such proficiency in teaching leaders how to optimize the provision of feedback can be conveyed through leadership Lunch 'N' Learns.

In these educational, peer-to-peer sessions, role model leaders can share success stories of what they implemented and the results that followed.

As an example, I had a new leader who took very seriously the importance we placed on the provision of feedback to our employees. She shared that when she held her initial performance conversation with a particular employee and thanked her for her role model accomplishments, this tenured employee burst out into tears. Although this employee had worked within the same department for years, no previous leader had ever taken the time to express with purpose that she was making a positive difference. Regrettably, this star employee had never received prior feedback that her work was outstanding, nor that she was greatly valued and appreciated. What a travesty. Yet what an opportunity this leader and her employees had for the future with open, systematic performance conversations!

I have consistently observed a direct correlation between the quality of performance feedback our employees received and the quality of the work they delivered. As gracious leaders, it is not only our responsibility, but also our opportunity and our joy, to ensure our employees receive the high quality, systematic feedback they need, want, and deserve.

Mid-Year Performance Conversations
I am a big fan of The Studer Group (Studer), as I have had the opportunity to work for an organization that engaged Studer to help drive improvements in the patient experience.

Within his book, *Hardwiring Excellence*, author and healthcare industry icon Quint Studer stresses the importance of providing strategic feedback to employees. One of the processes he advocates is called High Middle Low ™ Performer Conversations. My teams have utilized an adaptation of the High Middle Low (HML) process and found the results to be stunning. Six months after the annual performance evaluation and conversation, we expected our leaders to categorize their employees as high performers, middle performers, or low performers by answering a series of questions about each staff member's performance.

Each manager was then held accountable to have a short, yet meaningful, one-on-one meeting with every employee within the respective span of control. The managers held conversations based upon the following messaging:

High Performers: Thank the employee for his or her great work. Reinforce specifically how the employee serves as a role model. Ask what the employee wants to accomplish professionally in three years so the manager can support the employee's growth. The goal of the High Performer Conversation is to re-recruit your best employees.

Middle Performers: Tell the employee what he or she does well. Thank the employee for great work in specific areas. Then tell the employee definitive actions necessary for the employee to be more effective. Ask how you can support the employee's efforts to become more effective. The goal of the Middle Performer Conversation is to move middle performers to high performers.

Low Performers: Tell the employee specifically what he or she needs to do to improve performance and if improvement is not seen quickly, the employee will not get to stay with the organization. This should not be a surprise conversation as it is expected the manager has already counseled the employee about the need for improvement. The goal of the Low Performer Conversation is to move the low performers up to middle performers or out of the organization with proper guidance from HR.

As we initially introduced the concept of mid-year performance conversations, once again those managers with large spans of control voiced concerns about the time requirements. However, not only did they find a way to bring this concept to life by making these discussions a top priority, but these managers also became huge fans of the process and referred to the results as transformational.

And after we had implemented the process for a few cycles, we found employees would actually seek out their managers to schedule these meetings. They were eagerly anticipating the feedback they would receive through their one-on-one mid-year performance conversations.

We saw amazing results as high performers wanted to stay and grow within our organization, middle performers inquired as to what they needed to do differently to be more effective, and the number of poor performers declined because they either improved their performance or were "encouraged" to find other opportunities outside of the organization.

The Need to Be Brilliant at the Basics
The longer I have had the blessing of leading, the more amazed I have become about the number of organizations that are not brilliant at organizational basics such as properly conducted performance evaluations or systematic accountability and feedback processes. In this regard, many organizations are still in their leadership infancy.

Just know that now is the time for your organization to function more like a mature adult by implementing key business disciplines. You can start by being brilliant at the basics within your own area of responsibility. Through ensuring the use of proper business processes, you will be better able to make the most of your human capital on your journey to peak performance.

Gracious leaders must be role models in providing feedback to their employees with kind candor and grace. A proactive culture in which feedback is systematic and viewed as a *gift* should be fostered. After all, our employees are the most treasured assets that will ever be entrusted to us as leaders.

Learning How Not to Provide Feedback

It is important to note that in our professional roles we will no doubt have many opportunities to learn from others about how we want to lead. Unfortunately, we will also have opportunities to learn about how we *don't* want to lead.

Based upon my experience in receiving harsh feedback, as discussed within Chapter 14, I have chosen to use kind candor and grace when I share feedback with others and as I coach my leaders. Make no mistake about it; my feedback is clear, and it is candid, but it is also conveyed in a kind manner.

Feedback should be forthright, *and* it can and should be conveyed in a respectful manner at the right time and place. After all, as gracious leaders, the feedback that we provide to our employees should be a *gift* and not a *gotcha*.

Conversation Starters for Your Team

1. What actions will you take to be more effective in providing ongoing feedback to your employees?

2. What specific steps should your organization take to be more effective in providing systematic feedback to all employees?

3. What is your perception of how your direct reports feel about the quality of the feedback you provide to them? Pose the same question to your direct reports. Compare the feedback you receive from your direct reports to your own perceptions. What steps will you take to address any gaps and ensure the impact of the feedback is optimized?

4. What specific steps will you take to ensure your direct reports' performance evaluations and associated performance conversations are consistently thorough and meaningful?

5. What systematic improvements should be made in your organization's performance management processes to ensure that consistent, meaningful feedback is provided to all your employees?

Show employees how much
you care by role modeling
servant leadership.

Chapter 16

Gracious Leaders are Compassionate

I n the Foreword, Mike Slubowski referenced this famous quote from Theodore Roosevelt: "People don't care how much you know until they know how much you care."

One particular mentor stands out in my mind as someone who role modeled the importance of being a caring and compassionate leader. Not only did Aubrey Patterson help me stretch, learn, and grow as he taught me to be comfortable being uncomfortable, he also is one of the most compassionate leaders for whom I have ever worked.

I shall never forget that Mr. Patterson came to the hospital to check on me when my baby died. While this action may sound like a seemingly small act of kindness, it meant the world to me at that time of despair.

Mr. Patterson's wife, Ruby Kathryn, appeared at my house a few days after the baby's death. She shared with me a special book called *Hinds Feet on High Places*. And, she gave me a beautiful stained glass window that, to this day, I hold very dear. Inscribed on the stained glass window are the words "In Thee, Oh Lord, do I put my trust" [Psalm 31:1].

And after I left the bank to work for NMMC, it was Mr. Patterson who was among the first to congratulate me on the birth of my two daughters.

Not just any boss (and his wife) would show this kind of compassion to his or her employees. But Mr. Patterson was not just any boss. He was, and continues to be, a special leader. He made a deep imprint upon my leadership convictions, and I learned from him firsthand the importance for leaders to be compassionate. He also inspired me to be available and approachable to my employees. I count it among my greatest blessings to have served under his leadership.

As such, I have always been grateful for opportunities to show care and compassion to those whom I have had the joy of leading. To provide an example, it was a blessing when Fred from Environmental Services would stop me in the hallway to chat as I was making my rounds. One day, Fred shared that his wife had been diagnosed with cancer. He asked me to pray for her.

In following Mr. Patterson's footsteps, I was purposeful in asking Fred about his wife each subsequent time I saw him. We celebrated together when Fred shared his wife's health was improving.

I will forever remember a time that one of our front line Environmental Services employees experienced a significant surgery. I came into the hospital over the weekend to see her. Her beautiful smile said it all when I entered her room to check on her progress.

Derivatives of these stories could be replayed with Nancy, John, or Susan. What I learned from these experiences was that each time I reached out to support my staff with compassion at their times of greatest need, I was the one who received great joy.

Thank you, Mr. Patterson, for inspiring me to be more than just a boss. Thank you for inspiring me to be a gracious, caring, and compassionate leader.

Caring for Your Employees by Knowing Them

When MCSA was celebrating our 100th anniversary, our Leadership Team decided to revisit our history and heritage. In so doing, we sought to reground ourselves in leadership principles that were at the foundation of our hospital's origin.

As a part of this process, I asked our managers to identify the leaders who had the greatest impact upon St. Ann's between its founding in 1908 and its 100th anniversary in 2008. While the names of many individuals were offered, there was a prevailing theme as to *why* these leaders were impactful in such a special manner.

Over and over we heard "These leaders knew us; they really knew us."

The fact that leaders knew and cared about the employees took precedent over any leader's vision for the future, any administrative competencies, or any other stated attribute. Knowing and caring about employees was woven into the tapestry of St. Ann's. As a leadership team, we felt it was prime time to recommit to this legacy of caring that our founding order of nuns and administrative predecessors had established.

With 1,900 employees working on a 24/7/365 basis, and with 700 physicians and 300 volunteers, I cannot tell you that our C-Suite leaders knew the names of every employee and partner. What I can say, however, was that we did our very best to talk with all our employees, physicians, and volunteers when we were rounding, and we took the time to ask them about their families or special interests. And, we did try to remember as many of their names as possible.

In addition to expecting the leaders and managers throughout the hospital to know their employees, we also expected them to know what was going on in their lives and to support them accordingly.

How Do Your Employees Know That You Care?
In the book *The Three Signs of a Miserable Job*, author Patrick Lencioni stresses three important factors about employees to ensure a highly engaged work force.

1. Employees want to know they are making a difference and that their jobs matter to someone.

2. Employees want to know how much of a difference they are making.

3. Employees want to know their employer cares about them as a whole person and not just for what they do at work.

One way to help employees know you care about them is to incorporate the right questions into new employee orientation. We discussed this process in Chapter 6. In particular, we asked employees to share with us what they loved to do when they were *not* at work.

On an ongoing basis, you might also consider asking your managers to share with you on a systematic basis the important life events their staff members are experiencing so you can express your interest, congratulations or condolences. Life events my staff wanted to celebrate have ranged from weddings and the arrival of new babies and grandchildren to graduations and, from time to time, amazing accomplishments. As an example, one employee's son was named the Big Ten Conference Freshman Gymnast of the Week on multiple weeks during his first year in college. That certainly was a reason to celebrate!

Caring Through Service
Throughout the years, I have found it to be very helpful to show our

employees how much their leaders cared by *role modeling servant leadership*. We made it a routine practice at one health system for our leadership team to serve meals to employees during appreciation events and other special events we held for employees on all shifts.

I shall never forget one particular Christmas evening when I received a message around 9 p.m. that the third-shift cook had "called off." As a result, our night employees, who were already sacrificing by working on a holiday, were now going without the availability of an onsite evening meal.

My daughter and I literally drove all over town looking for snacks we could provide to the staff. As you can imagine, essentially every store was closed. We ultimately cleaned out all the Whitman's Sampler candy that a 24-hour drug store had on its shelves. Then my daughter and I, along with the nursing supervisor, delivered the candy at midnight to all the open departments. I offered my sincere apology we had failed to provide them with their holiday meal, and I promised such circumstances would not again occur.

While the employees were disappointed to miss their holiday evening meal, they also were appreciative we had made the effort to show we cared and offered the sweet treats as a small gesture of kindness.

Compassion for the Vulnerable

Another way you can show how much you care for your employees is through making provisions for your most vulnerable team members. What is your organization doing to help those hard-working employees who need assistance with basic life needs?

Our employee-led, Colleague Engagement Council at MCSA (See Chapter 10 regarding matching passion with purpose) initiated an annual holiday event called Annie's Toy Shop. Through this special event, our employees from throughout the hospital donated toys, warm clothing, gift cards, and more, so that every child or grandchild of our needy employees would have a happy Christmas morning. There were more heart-warming stories than I could possibly convey, but I can't resist sharing at least one such account.

The son of one of our nurse managers decided to forego his own presents so our neediest children might have a Merry Christmas. Through this young man's selflessness, several bicycles were purchased. When one of our cardiologists heard about the boy's generosity, he told his partners and they, along with their group's employees, spread the love even farther by donating more than 25 bicycles and helmets—a tradition they have since continued.

A similar giving spirit was present during Back to School seasons when this same leadership council coordinated the donation of much-needed school supplies for the children and grandchildren of our neediest employees. The spirit of caring was certainly alive and well at our hospital, as our team members were clearly living examples that "It is more blessed to give than to receive" [Acts 20:35].

As a leader, you will inevitably find yourself in situations in which you will make important, but potentially difficult and unpopular, decisions. I cannot stress enough how much it matters for employees to believe their leaders have compassion and really do care about them. This compassion results in employees having faith that their employers will act in their best interest in the good times as well as in the not-so-good times.

Gracious leaders must be both purposeful and consistent in showing employees how much they really care. It's not difficult. Just take a little time to look for opportunities to sincerely ask how your employees are doing and give them the chance to share their challenges and life events that are important to them.

There's No Place Like Home

During my tenure at MCSA, a new competing hospital was opening. This organization was aggressively recruiting nurses from one of our specialty units. They were offering attractive salary increases with a less stressful workload. Twelve of our nurses left our organization, which represented a significant loss for this team because specialty unit orientation is a long and time-consuming process.

Several months after these 12 nurses left, *all* of them wanted to come home to MCSA.

One of the nurses shared she did not feel the same sense of caring at the new hospital that their unit enjoyed at MCSA. She referenced there was an illness in her family and her new manager at the other hospital didn't seem to care. The nurse shared further her belief that her manager at St. Ann's would have worked her shifts for her if that had been required so she could attend to her family crisis.

While I am not inferring that leaders can always do the job of their employees, this story beautifully illustrates how the compassion of a leader can result in employee loyalty, employee retention and, in this case, employee return.

Gracious leaders are compassionate and caring leaders and, based upon the example set by Aubrey Patterson, the imprint they leave may well last forever.

Conversation Starters for Your Team

1. What actions will you take to demonstrate to your employees you really know them?

2. What actions will you take to demonstrate to your employees you consistently care about them?

3. What systematic programs and processes have been implemented within your organization to support your employees in their time of greatest need? What specific steps should be taken to optimize the compassion shown to your employees?

Notes

Take the time to be a gracious
and grateful leader by openly
praising great performances.

Chapter 17

Gracious Leaders are Grateful

G racious leaders are grateful as they are quick to express their appreciation for excellent work.

Early in my career, I received at home a short, handwritten note from my CEO.

Dear Janet,

Thank you for your great work. You are a valued member of our team, and I appreciate you.

Sincerely,

Sam

The power of a simple "Thank You" note, purposefully written, can be profound. Such notes can be likened unto the cheers of raving fans at football and basketball games. Even though I was already working tirelessly for this CEO, his simple, yet sincere, expression of gratitude made me want to do even more.

In building a culture in which gratitude can facilitate positive employee engagement, it is important to hold leaders accountable for praising the great work of their employees. As covered within Chapter 12, I have required my leaders to complete a periodic accountability report. Within this report, I expected our managers to share specifics regarding someone they wanted to recognize for their extraordinary efforts.

I promised our leaders that if they would take the time each month to find someone who had gone above and beyond the call of duty, I would make the time at nights or on weekends to send personal "Thank You" notes to the homes of these employees.

"Thank You" notes represent an easy and gratifying way to help employees fully embrace the Head-Heart Connection. In so doing, you can reinforce to your employees your awareness of and your gratitude for the meaningful work they do.

The Importance of Strategic, Systematic Recognition

When I initially introduced the expectation for our leaders to participate in strategic recognition by systematically identifying individuals who deserved to be praised, I experienced some resistance from a few managers. They expressed concern that by singling out one employee for accolades, the other staff persons might feel left out and have hurt feelings.

I assured these leaders that if every employee was truly going above and beyond the call of duty, we would find enough "Thank You's" to go around! I kindly and candidly let them know I was counting on them to identify at least one person each month for recognition.

A few leaders were also wary because they said *it would take time* to look for employees who were doing great work.

Think about that for a moment.

Concern was expressed that it would take time to find great work, but we always seem to make the time for dealing with negative staff members. What's wrong with that picture?

The introduction of a specific accountability to focus upon the positives as opposed to the negatives was an important cultural shift for our organization. While we were absolutely committed to deal with poor performers in short order, no longer were we going to allow the negativity of a few bad actors to take a disproportionate share of our minds, our time, or our culture.

The leaders and managers ultimately and enthusiastically embraced the challenge for strategic, systematic recognition. They started feeling great pride as they shared the amazing stories about all their employees had done to go above and beyond the call of duty ... indeed, to go the extra mile.

And many of the leaders started replicating the process of recognizing their role model employees by sending them handwritten "Thank You" notes. Some managers began to acknowledge their superstar employees during staff meetings. Others started featuring recognition bulletin boards within their respective departments to spread the word about all that their employees were doing to go above and beyond the call of duty.

The Simplicity and the Power of Thank You

The "Thank You" notes I wrote to employees were simple. While each communiqué was unique, an example of a typical note is shown as follows. I was intentional in including the supervisor's name within each note so the employee would clearly see that his or her boss had praised the extra mile efforts directly to me.

Dear Mary,

Jane Smith (supervisor's name) shared with me that you recently went the Extra Mile.

I understand that you and a colleague personally bought clothes for a homeless patient to take with him when he was discharged from our hospital.

I cannot thank you enough for your selfless act of kindness. I am sure that this patient will remember you for many years to come.

Thank you, Mary, for going the Extra Mile for this patient and for all the patients and families that you serve.

Sincerely,

Janet Meeks
MCSA President

Each month, I sent more than 50 handwritten notes to employees, physicians, or volunteers to express gratitude for their outstanding service.

After beginning the process of systematically sending "Thank You" notes, what happened next was nothing short of remarkable. I started *receiving* "Thank You" notes for having written "Thank You" notes. Seriously!

Employees would frequently stop me in the hall and express gratitude for the handwritten notes, oftentimes telling me they had put the notes on their refrigerators or their families had read the notes and were "so proud" of their loved ones.

Why did we receive this amazing response?

Because our employees were *starving* to know they were making a difference. In an era of technological dominance, handwritten expressions of gratitude speak much more loudly than a perceived "cut and paste" email. Emails simply do not convey a personalized touch. While they are quick and easy, they are not considered to be as sincere as a handwritten note.

Employees told me frequently they knew I was busy and it took time for me to send them a handwritten note. This made them feel *very* special.

Almost two years after I left my role as President of MCSA, I received an email on LinkedIn from a former nurse manager. She shared she still carries around in her nurse's bag the "Thank You" note I had written to her many years ago.

Need I say more? Oftentimes at work and at home we will discover that the little things in life are what really matter most. Who would have thought that simple "Thank You" notes would have had such a significant, positive impact? Gratitude was starting to go viral on our campus!

The passion for expressing gratitude was certainly taking flight, and it was clear that strategic, systematic recognition was becoming a vitally important part of our organizational culture.

Celebrating Great Work
To build upon a culture of positivity and gratitude, we began to invite to our monthly leadership team meetings those employees, physicians, or volunteers who had gone the extra mile in a truly extraordinary manner. Following our opening reflections, we started each meeting with a dedicated period of recognition and celebration.

We brought to the front of the room those individuals who were to be honored, and we asked their managers to share the stories about what these employees, physicians, or volunteers had done that had made a profound difference.

I reinforced in an individualized manner what each honoree's actions had meant to the patients, families, or co-workers. I thanked the honorees and presented each of them with a simple, yet personalized, certificate. The employees, physicians, and volunteers received resounding applause and sometimes standing ovations, depending upon the perceived impact of their actions.

On countless occasions, the honored individuals would cry tears of joy as their managers proudly shared the stories of how they had made a profound difference.

Sometimes the employees would bring their spouses, parents, children, and even their grandchildren. Physician group members would often attend if one of their partners was being recognized. To the individuals who were being honored, this recognition of the positive difference they had made was a big deal. And it was, indeed, a *very* big deal.

Over the course of time, expressing gratitude for excellence became such an integral part of our culture that the recognition ceremony would often consume an hour of our monthly leadership meetings. There were times when I wondered if we were recognizing too much. Then I quickly came to my senses and dismissed that ridiculous thought.

If so many employees, physicians, and volunteers were caring enough to make sacrifices for those whom we served, then the least we could do as leaders was to ensure we gave those superstars due recognition.

Over the years, I found only a few employees did not feel comfortable with public recognition during our Leadership Team meetings. In those cases, we would make the time to speak in private with these individuals. Regardless of the venue that was most comfortable for our honorees, we never wanted to miss an opportunity to thank our staff in a manner that was most meaningful to them.

Limitless Return on Investment

As leaders, we live in times of tight resources along with technology's dominant role in communications. Taking the time to be a gracious and grateful leader by openly praising great performances is one of your most important and long lasting opportunities.

The cost of paper for "Thank You" notes and certificates, coupled with a small amount of postage, is completely immaterial. However, the goodwill that is garnered among your key stakeholders by sincerely and purposefully saying "Thank you" is immeasurable.

Employees want (and deserve) to know they are making a positive difference. Through openly and freely expressing gratitude to employees, gracious leaders can keep the Head-Heart Connection alive and well in every employee's work day.

As gracious leaders, thanking those who are doing the real work on the front line is not only our duty, it is also likely to be among our most gratifying and impactful opportunities to serve.

Gracious leaders are grateful leaders. After all, they know that the seemingly small expressions of kindness like "Thank you" are among the really big things in life that matter most.

Conversation Starters for Your Team

1. What specific steps will you take to ensure your employees feel consistently appreciated and valued?

2. What specific steps will you take to be more purposeful in recognizing the great work of your employees on a consistent basis?

3. What processes exist within your organization to ensure leaders are accountable for identifying and recognizing employees who are going above and beyond the call of duty? What specific actions will you take to improve your own effectiveness in ensuring accountability for the recognition of great work?

4. If you were the CEO of your organization, what specific processes would you implement to ensure the recognition of great work is engrained within your organizational culture? What specific steps would you take to incorporate recognition as a systematic component of your leaders' daily responsibilities?

PART III

MAKING IT REAL

Employee engagement
is a driving force in
optimizing and sustaining
organizational performance.

Chapter 18

Gracious Leadership— Is it Soft Stuff?

A t one point in my career, shortly after we had introduced Triple A Leadership (Accountability, Alignment, and Acknowledgement, as covered in Chapter 12), our managers were working diligently to bookend greatly elevated levels of employee accountability with purposeful acknowledgement (feedback and recognition).

As we were coaching our leaders to embrace strategic, systematic recognition, one of the more tenured leaders asked to meet privately with me.

At the appointed time, this individual entered my office, sat down at the opposite end of the table with crossed arms and said the following:

"I just need to tell you that I disagree with how you are leading this organization with all of the soft stuff."

The leader elaborated further a disbelief in the need for or the value of recognition.

I thanked the leader for sharing these convictions. I then shared with kind candor that this was a situation in which we were going to have to agree to disagree. I encouraged the leader to rethink the position that had been voiced, and I encouraged the individual to come along with us in embracing recognition as an important leadership philosophy.

Then I shared that if the leader could not find a way to support these efforts, I would respect the individual's decision to make other arrangements.

After a few months, the leader decided to leave the organization.

Recognition is Strategic

Being a gracious leader by using recognition does not mean you are soft. It means you are *strategic*. In fact, you can be a more effective leader if you recognize well, and the data prove it.

Adrian Gostick and Chester Elton share in *The Carrot Principle* the results of a 10-year study of 200,000 managers and employees.

The authors state: "According to the data, companies in the highest quartile of recognition of excellence report an operating margin of 6.6 percent, while those in the lowest quartile report 1 percent."

Also from *The Carrot Principle*, Karen Endresen of The Jackson Organization shared: "Up until this study, the link between recognition and financial performance was largely anecdotal ... Recognition was considered by some to be an emotional afterthought ... This study took recognition results from myth to reality—from the soft side of business to a proven business essential."

David Novak is the co-founder and retired Chairman and CEO of Yum! Brands. He is also the founder of OGO (O Great One!), a brand dedicated to helping people through the power of recognition. According to Mr. Novak in a May 9, 2016, article within *Harvard Business Review*, "We need to recognize the tremendous value people bring to their work, regardless of their role in the organization. Recognition isn't just about implementing employee programs to check them off a list; it's about bringing out the best in people and improving your company's bottom line."

Employee Engagement in Driving Results
Also sometimes rebuffed as "soft stuff," employee engagement has been proven time and time again to be a driving force in optimizing and sustaining organizational performance.

In a March 22, 2013, article in *Harvard Business School Working Knowledge* entitled "Pulling Campbell's Out of the Soup," Dina Gerdeman explores the achievements of Campbell's Soup under the leadership of Douglas Conant, the company's president and CEO.

According to Gerdeman, "Campbell was in rough shape when Conant joined the company in 2001 … By the time Conant was recruited, the company's share price had dropped from a high of $60 in 1998 to $30." She quoted Conant, who said, "We had a toxic culture. People were understandably jaundiced with management. It was hard for me to imagine that we could inspire high performance with no employee engagement."

The Campbell CEO further shared, "We needed to reach employees on four levels: People needed to make a living, they needed to feel loved, they needed to learn, and they needed to feel like they were part of something special and leave a legacy behind. Hitting on those four cylinders, we were able to create a very powerful culture."

In a June 23, 2009, article entitled "How Employee Engagement Turned Around Campbell's" by *Forbes* contributor Terry Waghorn, Conant shared the following during an interview, "To win in the marketplace, we believe you must first win in the workplace. I'm obsessed with keeping employee engagement front and center and keeping up energy around it."

The numbers certainly speak volumes regarding Campbell's outstanding results. As Gerdeman noted, "For the six years preceding July 2010, Campbell's cumulative total shareholder return was 64 percent, nearly five times the 13 percent return of the S&P 500." It has been reported that while under Conant's leadership, Campbell's sales, earnings, and market share increased nearly every year.

And while Gerdeman shared a variety of strategies that Conant utilized to affect this dramatic turnaround in culture and performance, I would like to point out that during his 10 years as CEO, he wrote 30,000 "Thank You" notes to a base of 20,000 employees.

Kevin Kruse, founder and CEO of Leadx.org, *New York Times* bestselling author, and an *Inc.* 500 entrepreneur, wrote an October 25, 2016, Leadx article entitled, "How the Engagement-Profit Chain Leads to a 5X Higher Stock Price." Within the article, Mr. Kruse shared, "In a 2009 study conducted by Kenexa, the most engaged companies had five times higher total shareholder return (over five years) than the least engaged companies. In another study, conducted by Towers Perrin in 2011, companies with engaged employees were found to have 6 percent higher net profit margins."

Within the article, Mr. Kruse expressed his belief about the Engagement-Profit Chain which was "based on the classic 'Service Profit Chain' first described by Jim Jeskett and Earl Sasser. The Engagement-Profit Chain model details how the discretionary effort of a workforce triggers a series of beneficial actions."

"Engaged Employees lead to …

Higher Service, Quality, and Productivity, which lead to …

Higher Customer Satisfaction, which leads to ...

Increased Sales (repeat business and referrals), which leads to ...

Higher levels of profits, which lead to ...

Higher shareholder returns (i.e., stock price)."

There are many other examples of articles that substantiate the position that when employees feel they are appreciated, respected, and valued—and when they are doing work about which they are passionate—they are more likely to be engaged, loyal, and productive. And their employers, customers, and shareholders are the beneficiaries as these companies are more likely to excel in customer satisfaction and profitability.

From Research to Reality

In addition to all I have learned through researching the topics of leadership, positive work culture, and employee engagement as related to team performance, I have personally seen extraordinary outcomes within organizations in which I have served. The secret sauce is to assure that *all* the key ingredients of Gracious Leadership are *consistently* practiced.

During my nine years at MCSA, my greatest joy was to have the honor of building and empowering a fabulous team as we collectively transformed a struggling community hospital into a vibrant, award-winning regional medical center.

I shared with you in Chapter 4 that in 2006, the team at MCSA had tall mountains to climb as an operational turnaround was needed. It could have been easy for our Leadership Team to doubt its own ability to drive the type of change required to achieve excellence.

To the contrary, this team embraced the power of believing. Instead of remaining a community hospital with the worst patient satisfaction scores in central Ohio, this team chose to dream big about becoming a regional medical center with excellence across the balanced scorecard.

These leaders learned to believe in themselves and the potential of their employees. They believed we could set the bar high, and that we could reach and achieve better results together than anyone had ever imagined. They believed in the art of possibility, and in so doing, they started leading like they had never led before.

The results that followed were nothing short of remarkable.

By 2015, MCSA had achieved a very strong bottom line. Patient satisfaction had increased by 20-plus percent. The employees were engaged with a keen focus on excellent patient care, and national quality awards had been earned.

Medical staff, administrative and clinical leaders worked in tandem on important quality and safety initiatives. Physicians were valued partners as they led the introduction of sophisticated medical and surgical services in a collaborative and supportive manner.

MCSA received Leapfrog Grade A for outstanding quality, and a Healthgrades distinction was earned for being in the top 5 percent of the nation's hospitals.

These transformative results speak for themselves. And it is my honor to give *all the credit* for these amazing achievements to the dedicated team of administrative, clinical, and physician leaders and, of course, to the wonderful employees and volunteers at MCSA.

Just as the CEO of Campbell's Soup talked about the importance of his employees' needing to make a living, feel loved, learn, and feel like they were a part of something special and leave a legacy behind, so also did the people of MCSA.

Clearly, the MCSA leaders made a transformational difference. They cared *for* and *about* our patients, employees, physicians, volunteers, and community. They believed our people could make a difference, and then they led them to do so. What a legacy they have left!

My role was simply to see and unleash their potential so they could lead like they had never led before.

Gracious Leadership is *not at all* about soft stuff. Much to the contrary, Gracious Leadership is about getting the right results in the right manner … for Gracious Leadership clearly represents the intersection of ultimate respect and optimal outcomes.

As SAS CEO James Goodknight said, "Treat people like they make a difference and they will."

Conversation Starters for Your Team

1. Do you personally believe recognition and employee engagement are soft stuff? If so, take some time to research the impact of recognition and employee engagement on the performance of organizations. Through your research, look for examples of organizations in which corporate performance was suboptimal due to disengaged employees or the lack of established recognition processes.

2. What did you specifically learn within this chapter to substantiate the reality that recognition and engagement are strategic?

3. What steps will you take to communicate to your team the strategic importance of recognition (gratitude) and engagement, as well as the other key ingredients of Gracious Leadership?

4. Triple A Leadership (Accountability, Alignment, and
    Acknowledgement) are important building blocks for sustained
    organizational success. Discuss with your team how *all* three elements
    of Triple A Leadership are required to optimize organizational
    performance within a fully respectful work environment.

5. Describe the specific actions you will take to implement Triple A
    Leadership within your team.

When your organization's
fully respectful, peak performance
culture is just right,
you will know it.

Chapter 19

Caramel Cake and Culture

Throughout this book, I have shared some of my childhood experiences from growing up in Mississippi during the racial unrest of the 1960s.

I shall be forever grateful to have had a father who was ahead of his time. He shared such passion that everyone is to be respected equally and that leaders must do what's right, fair and just—even, and especially when it is not popular.

From the Eyes of a Child

I have a wide range of memories from my childhood. For example, in my small hometown of Carthage (with a population of 3,000 people at the time), I remember being surrounded by adults who told me I could do anything in life I wanted to do and could be anything I wanted to become.

I remember my Kindergarten teacher, Mr. E. O. White, who instead of stressing my error by telling me I was writing my N's backwards, lovingly took his hand and placed it over mine to guide me in how to write an N the correct way.

I remember being in church every time the doors were open. I am grateful for the positive female mentors who gave of their time and influence to ensure I would be grounded in my faith, which has carried me through the valleys of my life.

I remember happily riding my bicycle to my best friend's house. And, I remember when my parents one day abruptly refrained from allowing me to play with another good friend at her family's farm. At the time, I had no idea that my parents were protecting me from potential harm because this friend's father was a leader in the Ku Klux Klan.

I remember walking to town and enjoying a freshly squeezed orange-ade at Mr. Cliff Bailey's soda fountain inside of his drug store. And I remember watching in horror from the windows of that same drug store as Klansmen in their scary, white hooded uniforms would parade around the courthouse square and loudly summon through their megaphones for the people of Carthage to attend the hate rally they would be hosting on Saturday night.

I remember looking out of our bathroom window with my brother and mother to see the very rare snow flurries as they glistened against the outdoor flood light. And I also remember that from time to time my brother and I would peer with curiosity out of the other bathroom window at night, noting an unknown car that was routinely parked close to our house. We later learned that the car was there to protect our family because of our father's proactive stance on Civil Rights.

I remember when mass integration occurred how our community became divided as never before. A new private school was opened, and half of the white kids, including close friends, left the public school system to attend Leake Academy.

Our family remained loyal to the public schools, and my brother and I made the daily drive together as we attended the previous "all black" high school during the first semester of mass integration.

Seeking Commonality in Tumultuous Times

I remember that while things felt awkward for the students when mass integration first occurred, I also recall that we students seemed to be searching for common ground that might lead us to a glimpse of unity within a town that had been deeply divided.

For many of us, it was the sport of basketball that brought us together. During basketball season, black and white families would unite to cheer their hearts out for our newly formed teams. I remember the closeness my team members and I experienced as we focused on our coach's game plan. We knew that we would have each other's backs and we would do our very best collectively to bring pride to our community through the victories that together we would strive to achieve.

I remember that while things weren't at all perfect during those tumultuous times, it seemed that those of us who found ourselves at this important crossroads in history were earnestly looking for commonality. And I am grateful to have learned from my parents that, as human beings, *all* of us really are much more alike than we are different.

I remember that when my father died, black and white residents came to the funeral home to pay their respects to a very special man. My dad was described at his death within an editorial column of our local newspaper, *The Carthaginian*, as "An Uncommon Man." Indeed he was an uncommon man, as he was either loved or hated because of his stance on equality and respect.

Family Traditions

My family *loved* Ole Miss football. It was a true family affair. As a matter of fact, I attended my first Ole Miss football game one month and one day *before* I was born—the 1955 Sugar Bowl.

As a young child, I remember our family's revered tradition of tailgating in The Grove at Ole Miss on most weekends in the fall. Back in those days, there was room for cars to park in The Grove and for the little ones to run around and play freely.

I remember the very day that my father explained to me what "first and ten" meant, and I remember seeing Archie Manning lead the Rebels with his amazing athletic capabilities. I also recall feeling crushed in the moment when Archie Manning's arm was broken during the team's 1970 game in Oxford with the Houston Cougars.

And I remember Hattie Bell's Caramel Cake.

Any time that my family would tailgate at Ole Miss football games, and for that matter, any time we had a special family gathering, a Hattie Bell Caramel Cake would invariably be at the center of the table. The same was true for families throughout Carthage, as Hattie Bell Johnson was both loved as a wonderful person and equally revered as the best baker in our small town.

The Science and the "Art Part"

Many years later, my paternal grandmother, Mama Smith, gave me a cookbook that was published by her small church. I was ecstatic to see that within that tiny little cookbook was the recipe for Hattie Bell's Caramel Cake.

As a young adult, I desperately wanted to make a Hattie Bell Caramel Cake so that I might continue this important culinary tradition during my own young family's special events. All the key ingredients were clearly listed within the recipe.

Time and time again, I would faithfully follow the recipe's directions to make this amazing cake. Yet on many occasions, I would be incredibly frustrated in my failure to get the cake icing "just right." My journey of trial and error in making this dessert taught me that both *science* and *art* would be required to get the icing consistently to the desired consistency.

The science of the key ingredients remained the same with each attempt. Over time, however, I learned that it was the "art part" that would vary, as I would need to include abundant patience along with the right amounts of perseverance, persistence, and, of course, a little bit of love. And I learned that there would simply be no room for shortcuts to get the cake icing "just right."

Believe it or not, mastering the art of making a Hattie Bell Caramel Cake is very much like the journey to create a fully respectful, peak performance work culture. Both efforts require the science of precise key ingredients. For the Hattie Bell Cake, it is sugar, flour, butter, and more. For a fully respectful, peak performance work culture, all 13 key ingredients of Gracious Leadership must be included. For both the cake and culture, none of the key ingredients can be omitted.

Both the cake and a gracious, peak performance culture also require the "art part." They each call for the right mix of patience, persistence, perseverance, and love. Making a Hattie Bell Caramel Cake is really hard, and the same is certainly true in creating and sustaining a positive, highly effective culture.

There was a major difference, however, between my efforts to make a Hattie Bell Caramel Cake and my journey to be a gracious leader. Unlike this beloved dessert recipe that has been passed down through generations, when I began my leadership journey, the "key ingredients" for becoming a good and gracious, respectful and effective leader were not recorded in any one place.

To my knowledge, there was simply no recipe within any textbook or leadership book that clearly articulated the necessary steps required to become a respectful leader who would also expect consistent excellence and peak performance within a positive work environment.

And that is precisely why I decided to write this book.

Leadership That Withstands the Test of Time

The key ingredients of Gracious Leadership are not a fad that will be here today and gone tomorrow. Much to the contrary, these lessons of leadership and life were important in the past. These principles are sorely needed within our society, our government, and our places of work today. And no doubt, these leadership convictions will prospectively withstand the test of time.

To summarize the key ingredients of becoming a gracious leader as covered within Part II of this book, all 13 attributes of gracious leaders are critical "must haves." And, as with the Hattie Bell Cake, no shortcuts are allowed!

Gracious leaders are grounded in *respect* for all and value solid *relationships* of trust where leaders *listen with purpose and respond with care.*

Gracious leaders *see problems as opportunities* and *ask the right questions to empower the team* so they can *match the passion of the person with the purpose of the work.*

Gracious leaders *develop their people and are accountable* for themselves and the team.

Gracious leaders are *courageous* in always doing what is right, fair, and just.

Gracious leaders *seek feedback* for continuous improvement of self and of the organization and they *provide feedback* to their followers to maximize organizational potential.

Gracious leaders are *compassionate* by caring for their employees.

And gracious leaders are *grateful* as they understand the power of "Thank you."

Once you hold yourself accountable to the consistent application of Gracious Leadership's key ingredients, you then should teach these same convictions to the leaders who follow you, holding them accountable to the same high standards you have set for yourself.

As the principles of Gracious Leadership become second nature to you *and* to your team, you will find that *together* you are creating a work culture that is ripe for peak performance. In addition to the key ingredients of Gracious Leadership, just remember to add patience, persistence, perseverance, and a little bit of love. *When you get the culture "just right", you will know it*!

And about the Hattie Bell Caramel Cake … after years of many failed attempts, I finally mastered the recipe. Yet every time I make this special cake, I still have to remind myself that no shortcuts are permitted. In addition to the same key ingredients, I must always be artful in adding just the right amount of patience, persistence, perseverance and love.

Whether it's a Hattie Bell Caramel Cake or a gracious and respectful peak performance work culture, once you get it "just right", *you will absolutely know it*! And everyone who has a seat at the table with you will also know that it is *oh, so good*!

Conversation Starters for Your Team

1. What specific steps will your take to incorporate the key ingredients of Gracious Leadership within your own leadership style?

2. What peak performance outcomes could you possibly expect your team to accomplish when you are consistently serving as a role model of Gracious Leadership?

3. If you were the CEO of your organization, what peak performance outcomes could you possibly expect your organization to accomplish within one year, three years, and five years if all of your leaders serve as role models of Gracious Leadership?

4. What will be different about your team and its performance when you are consistently using the science of Gracious Leadership along with the *art part*? How will your team members know when the fully respectful, peak performance culture at your organization is "just right"?

Don't promote negative behaviors
of bad bosses by permitting them
through your silence.

Chapter 20

Gracious Leadership— Why Do Some Leaders Miss the Mark?

Have you ever wondered what would motivate a leader to be hateful, mean, nasty, or rude? Have you worked for someone who is sarcastic, unkind, surly, brusque, ungrateful, or unpleasant? These unflattering words can be found in the dictionary if you search for the definition of "ungracious."

Do you *really* want to work for or with a person who acts like that?

While these words may sound extreme, I sadly believe we still have too many people in high places in Corporate America and throughout our nation who are leading their teams with ungracious behaviors.

I recently asked several colleagues to describe the worst boss they have ever had. You know the type; it's "that" boss.

Some of the replies I received were as follow:

"My boss was such a bully. When he called, I was often afraid to answer the phone because I, along with my peers, never knew when

he was going to 'go off' on us. One day he was threatening me, and he even asked if I was willing to lose my job when I had done nothing wrong. That was the day that I came very close to leaving a job and an organization that I loved."

"My boss, a high-ranking leader in our organization, was well known for throwing people under the bus, passing the buck and 'putting people in their place.' While he was often ill-prepared for meetings, he would call out other team members and blame them for not doing assignments that were clearly his responsibility to complete as documented within the minutes. Of course, when it was time for public recognition, my boss was always the first in line for praise."

"My boss wouldn't listen to me when I brought forth legitimate concerns. Because this ongoing dysfunction ultimately made me feel that I was being taken for granted, I eventually developed a bad attitude as opposed to being a corporate cheerleader. This drove me to the point where I actually submitted my resignation to work for a competitor."

"My boss took credit for the work that I did. One time, my team and I had developed comprehensive recommendations for a very important strategic initiative. My boss took the completed document along with my cover letter and had his assistant retype the cover letter verbatim with the exception of having his assistant replace my name with his name. He then sent the proposal up the ladder to his boss. Needless to say, I was floored."

"My boss never gave us any feedback unless it was negative. Our work was never good enough for her."

Even a *temporary* boss can have long-lasting, negative repercussions as shared in the following story about a bad boss.

"During a leader transition, the direct reports of the departed

executive temporarily reported to another person on the executive team while a replacement was being recruited. For the team left behind, these types of transitions can be filled with feelings that are both negative (uncertainty, stress) and positive (excitement, promise) regarding the future. The temporary executive can play a significant role in how these feelings manifest within the team and the individuals.

In this case, the surrogate executive had a history of being tough, and not necessarily fair, coupled with a reputation of being unappreciative, unyielding, and intimidating. These characteristics were widely known and tolerated by others, generally due to favorable annual operating results of the organization. But, those positive organizational results certainly came at a cost to employee morale, engagement, growth, and personal effectiveness.

I'll never forget the first formal interaction in this temporary relationship. It was a very short encounter when the surrogate executive summoned everyone to a meeting. After a brief explanation of the process and the anticipated length of the temporary reporting relationship, the executive simply advised everyone would be wise to just keep their heads down ... so they don't get lopped off. Meeting over ... after only five minutes.

There were no mentions of teamwork or that we need everyone during this transition. No comments were made that "You will all be of great help to me and the organization," that "You all do great work," or "Please let me know how I can help you." There was no discussion of how we would be involved in the process of looking for a new executive; nothing. The implication was we were a burden, an inconvenience, another thing to do. And we may have been. But a gracious leader wouldn't let that show.

Not everyone survived the transition, including me; but it was my *choice, not the executive's. That was not a person or an organization in which I wanted to invest my personal contributions and growth. I found another organization, working with the same gracious leader for whom I had served before she left.*

Never looking back, I continue to be in my "new" organization over a decade later—learning, growing, and being challenged (and appreciated) in the contributions I am making."

Bryan Lufkin published an article in *BBC Capital* on June 21, 2017, the day that Travis Kalanick resigned as CEO of Uber. Within this article, "Six telltale signs of a toxic boss," Lufkin shared that Kalanick was pressured by investors to resign following months of scandals about sexual harassment, a macho culture, and the departure of senior executives. He reported that Kalanick's dramatic departure was a snapshot of one of the most stunning CEO roller-coaster stories in modern business history.

Lufkin identified some of the classic signs of toxic work culture that are all too common across many industries and that I heard directly from colleagues as they described "bad bosses."

- A boss who yells, bullies, or antagonizes

- A "success at all costs" philosophy

- Unfair treatment of workers

- A boss who is a control freak

- Absent management (i.e., a management that barely interacts with employees)

- Bad press

Altogether, the results of bad bosses can be disastrous. In fact, many corporations and other organizations may well be reaching a crisis of leadership.

A Crisis of Leadership

Turn on the television, surf the Internet, or look at your social media newsfeed, and you'll see that many organizations are facing an actual crisis of leadership.

Companies such as American Apparel and Uber were once heralded as leaders within their respective sectors. Yet because of the untenable actions and behaviors demonstrated by their CEOs, these companies have taken a hit to their performance and corresponding value.

Within a January 14, 2017, article in *The Atlantic* entitled "Goodbye American Apparel," Bouree Lam reported that "a bankruptcy court in Delaware approved an $88 million sale of the brand's intellectual property and manufacturing equipment. The company went from $633 million in sales, with over 200 stores in 20 countries, to two bankruptcy filings within two years. In the last three years of the company's life, American Apparel encountered huge debts, costly legal battles involving its founder, and a drop in sales." Lam quotes Mark Cohen, the director of retail studies at Columbia Business School, who said, "American Apparel is the best and worst of all things."

Leaders serve as role models for their followers, and young people clearly look up to leaders and aspire to be like them. As a result, today's ungracious leaders are fostering a long-term, negative impact through creating tomorrow's "bad bosses." In so doing, ungracious leaders are causing harm to a much broader circle of followers. The influence of bad leaders truly does represent the "worst of all things" in many walks of life.

Sadly, the crisis of leadership is much more pervasive than we care to imagine. Whether it's the CEO of a Fortune 500 company, a middle manager within a privately-held corporation, a director within a community non-profit, or the elected leader of an entire nation, why in the world is negative, ungracious, and disrespectful leadership tolerated?

The crisis of leadership is not limited to corporate organisms alone, but rather extends to other business, community, and governmental entities or any "collective body" in which leaders are leading and followers are following.

What is it that makes some leaders miss the mark?

Perhaps they learned bad habits from others at home or at work.

Perhaps no one gave them boundaries or confronted their bad behaviors due to the fear of retribution.

Perhaps these leaders have somehow achieved strong bottom lines in the short-term.

Perhaps some ungracious leaders think that by acting tough they are demonstrating strength. Yet down deep inside, these individuals may actually be very insecure, and they believe that by putting down others, they will lift themselves up.

Perhaps some of these leaders believe that their followers actually desire such negative antics.

Perhaps some of these leaders were simply good actors during the interview process and their true colors became obvious after the new job honeymoon was over. Or perhaps some of these individuals are simply not happy.

Why do some leaders miss the mark?

Perhaps it's, regrettably, because *we let them.*

Enabling Bad Bosses

In a June 20, 2017, issue of the academic journal *The Conversation,* authors Katina Sawyer and Christian Thoroughgood wrote an article entitled "Fixing a toxic culture like Uber's requires more than just a new CEO."

The authors state, "Our work on toxic leadership demonstrates how toxic, unethical, flawed, or otherwise ineffective leaders can do a lot of damage in organizations. But the damage can also run both ways. Susceptible followers, a lack of checks and balances, and other cultural elements can help create or reinforce bad leadership."

The authors identify two types of followers who are "likely to remain obedient to toxic leaders, turn a blind eye to their behavior, and even participate in the leader's destructive activities: conformers (individuals who are prone to obedience) and colluders (those who actively align themselves with toxic leaders)."

The authors believe that colluders "need to be rooted out and let go." They should not be allowed to stay because they share the same values and bad behaviors as a toxic leader. Conformers need to be retrained again and again and again to understand and to emulate the right behaviors that will be required within a healthy work culture.

I couldn't agree more!

As gracious leaders, we must understand that our own action or inaction will determine what will happen with a bad boss. In essence, *we have to own it.*

Irish Statesman Edmund Burke moved to London and served there as a member of Parliament for many years. He is often remembered for his profound statement, *"The only thing necessary for the triumph of evil is for good men to do nothing."*

Burke would tell us that to do nothing in the presence of toxic leaders allows the bad to win. Not OK! As gracious leaders, we cannot remain quiet and meek in the midst of bad bosses.

Can Bad Bosses Change?

I want to believe that bad bosses *can* change, but only *if* they understand their need for change, *and* if they *want* to change.

In Chapter 13, we talked about ways through which to confront a bully boss. If you know someone who leads in an ungracious manner, my hope is you will not be a conformer, but rather you will have the courage to make a positive difference by helping that person see his or her need to change for the better. Remember that silence is *not* golden!

Or if through our conversation you have been inspired to critique your own leadership style, may you be diligent in adopting the key ingredients of Gracious Leadership. Please do not allow yourself to become "that" boss and, in so doing, to lead to the ultimate decline of your organization and its people.

According to Mahatma Gandhi, "*You* must be the change you wish to see in the world." Will those whom you lead remember you as a good and gracious leader who facilitated the achievement of the right results within a fully respectful work environment? Or will you be remembered as "that" boss who taught your team how *not* to lead?

The opportunities are now yours to ponder.

Conversation Starters for Your Team

1. What are the top priority actions you will take as you begin to apply the key ingredients of Gracious Leadership?

2. What specific steps will you take to inspire other leaders to embrace the key ingredients of Gracious Leadership?

3. What are the top three actions you and your team should take to improve your collective effectiveness as gracious leaders? How will you hold each other accountable? How will you celebrate your successes?

4. What specific steps will you take to ensure you are not promoting ungracious, bully behaviors by permitting them through your silence?

The positive ripple effect
of your gracious leadership
carries great potential for many
generations to come.

Chapter 21

Lead Like You've Never Led Before

I t is with a humble heart that I thank you for joining me in this exploration of Gracious Leadership. I trust you have benefitted from the time we have spent together as we took a deep dive into the 13 key ingredients of Gracious Leadership.

I also trust that you will be inspired to live as a more gracious leader. May those who follow you learn from you and lead their respective teams to achieve optimal outcomes through ultimate respect.

I remember on many occasions at MCSA telling our leadership team that we all needed to lead like we had never led before.

When we were building our fabulous $110 million expansion as part of our facility's transformation into a regional medical center, we had many conversations to the effect that if all we did was to build pretty buildings, we would have failed as leaders.

Not only did we have to complete the construction on time and within budget, but we also had to advance our performance across our balanced scorecard. And for us to get to those outstanding results discussed in Chapter 18, we would have to step up and lead like we had never led before.

We had to count on our all our people more than ever ... our employees, our physicians, and our volunteers ... to remain committed to making every patient feel like he or she was the *only* person in our world.

And the key ingredients of Gracious Leadership had to be applied to achieve peak performance within a fully respectful work environment.

I am very pleased to share that our team accomplished the right results by leading with grace and by keeping the critical importance of the Head-Heart Connection front and center with our employees.

Our success as a team was made possible because our leaders were willing to buy into a new vision. They believed that *together* we could bring that vision to life. And they inspired our employees every day to understand they held the power to transform the lives of our patients through their seemingly small acts of kindness.

These leaders did indeed lead like they had never led before!

Now It's Your Turn
My goal is that you will now take some time to reflect upon *how* you lead.

Consider the key ingredients of Gracious Leadership and explore how you might improve upon your own leadership behaviors both at work and at home.

I hope that you will be inspired to act quickly as you decide what specific steps you will take to become a good and gracious leader.

- How will you show up differently every day?

- Who will you choose as an accountability partner to provide you with feedback as to whether or not you are consistently leading with goodness and with grace?

- How will you be purposeful in teaching others what you have learned about Gracious Leadership?

- What will you do to stop ungracious, toxic behaviors that may currently be tolerated?

- What will you do to create a culture of compassionate accountability in which peak performance is expected within a fully respectful work environment?

In short, what will *you* do to lead like you've never led before?

In this book, I have had the privilege of talking with great respect about several gracious leaders: Harry Jacobson, MD, Aubrey Patterson, Mike Slubowski, Dan Wilford and, of course, my parents.

I am incredibly blessed these individuals have made me a better leader. The legacy left by these professionals has been vast and will no doubt last for many years to come.

As a gracious leader, please know the positive ripple effect of *your* leadership also carries great potential to last for many generations to come. My hope is you, too, will leave a legacy of leading with goodness and with grace.

And now, gracious leader, it's your turn! *Go and lead like you've never led before!*

My Gracious Leadership Reflections

1. How will you show up differently every day as you aspire to be a Gracious Leader?

2. Who will you choose as an accountability partner to provide you with ongoing feedback as to whether you are consistently leading with goodness and with grace?

3. How will you be purposeful in teaching others what you have learned about Gracious Leadership?

4. What are your top areas of focus to create a culture of compassionate accountability in which peak performance can be achieved within a fully respectful work environment?

5. How will you demonstrate ultimate respect as you lead your team to accomplish optimal outcomes?

6. What specific steps will you take to stop toxic behavior?

7. What else will you do to lead like you've never led before?

We learn from others, and then perpetuate these lessons by teaching them to those who follow us.

Epilogue

During the past year, I have been blessed to have had the opportunity to write this book about Gracious Leadership. I'd like to extend my heartfelt gratitude to my husband, Richard D'Enbeau, for his encouragement and unwavering support throughout this journey.

My purpose in writing this book was quite simple: The principles of Gracious Leadership are timeless, and books last longer than people.

It was important that I capture the key ingredients of Gracious Leadership and share these lessons about leadership and life with the generations who will follow and who are inspired to embrace these convictions.

As I began the process of writing Gracious Leadership, I fondly relived some of my early career memories. I also had the opportunity to reconnect with four of my favorite leaders. This reunion of sorts proved to be an unanticipated gift.

As I pondered the lessons learned from Harry Jacobson, MD, Aubrey Patterson, Mike Slubowski and Dan Wilford, the more grateful I became for the life-at-large lessons these individuals independently taught me.

I was purposeful in reaching out to each of these Legacy Leaders to ask their permission to honor them by sharing within *Gracious Leadership* what they each had taught me about leadership and life. Without exception, each of these industry-leading professionals displayed extraordinary humility. This was no surprise. That's just who they are.

I still suspect that they don't fully realize the positive impact they each have had (and continue to have) on so many people. I'm just grateful I personally had an opportunity to say, "Thank you for believing in me and for helping to make me a better leader."

If my parents were still living, I would certainly share with them the same expression of gratitude ... except I would also include my heartfelt thanks for inspiring me to be the type of parent that my daughters, Meredith and Mallory, would want to follow. Ladies, I know that you are already paying it forward by teaching Gracie and Stella the baby steps of Gracious Leadership. Thank you for instilling within each of them the true meaning of respect and the importance of saying "Please" and "Thank you."

As leaders, we often hear about paying it forward. This is what we are supposed to do. We learn from others, and then we perpetuate these lessons by teaching them to those who follow us.

As my time with you in *Gracious Leadership* is coming to a close, I invite you to join me, not only in paying it forward, but also in *reaching back*. Take the time to reflect upon those leaders (formal or informal) who have helped you to believe that you can accomplish anything. Ponder those leaders who gave you stretch assignments or opportunities you never dreamed to be possible. Think about those leaders who believed in you and helped you to embrace your life's calling. These individuals are *your* Legacy Leaders.

And then take just a little time to reach back and express your gratitude to those leaders who paid it forward to you. I know it will mean the world to them.

And oh, by the way, reaching back in this manner to your Legacy Leaders is certainly the good and gracious thing to do!

Hattie Bell's Caramel Cake

1 cup butter
5 eggs
1 cup of milk
2 ½ tsp. baking power

2 ½ cups sugar
3 ½ cups flour
1 tsp. vanilla

Cream butter, add sugar, and beat until light and fluffy. Add whole eggs one at a time, beating well after each addition. Add vanilla to milk. Sift flour and baking powder. Add part of flour mixture, add milk and then remaining flour and beat until smooth. Pour batter into three greased and lightly floured 9-inch cake pans. Bake 30 minutes in preheated 375-degree oven.

Caramel Icing

3 ½ cups sugar
1 cup milk
½ pound butter

2 tbsp. white Karo
½ cup Cremora
1 tsp. vanilla

Mix sugar, Cremora, Karo, and milk in large pan. Cook for 5 minutes. Add ½ cup sugar that has been browned, cooking until it forms a soft ball when dropped into cold water. Add butter and vanilla and cook until butter dissolves. Beat until icing is right for spreading between layers, then beat until creamy for icing the remainder of the cake.

Mrs. Hattie Bell Johnson, Carthage

Author's Notes

I have passed along Hattie Bell's Caramel Cake recipe exactly as it was written in the New Hope Baptist Church Cook Book. This collection of favorite recipes was published to honor the American Revolution Bicentennial 1776–1976.

I will add a few clarifications. These steps represent the "art part."

- Be sure not to overcook the cake so that it will not be dry.

- Cook the icing in a 5 quart, non-stick pot. Use powdered Cremora. In addition to 3 ½ cups of sugar required in the recipe, brown ½ cup of sugar in a small, non-stick skillet during the time that the sugar, milk, Karo, and Cremora are cooking.

- I use a candy thermometer and cook the icing to 236–237 degrees, still applying the soft ball test that is required in the recipe.

- After adding the butter and vanilla to the icing, I beat the icing with a mixer until it reaches the right consistency to spread between layers. I then beat the icing by hand until it reaches a creamy consistency that is right for icing the remainder of the cake.

- Remember that no short cuts are allowed. Always use patience, persistence, perseverance and love to get the icing "just right."

Your Journey to Become a
Gracious Leader

As you begin your journey to become a gracious leader, I look forward to hearing about all you are learning and all you and your team have accomplished.

Be sure to celebrate your great work along the way. I especially invite you to share with your team your light bulb moments as you apply the key ingredients of Gracious Leadership. In so doing, you will encourage your team members to *join in the movement* to become gracious leaders.

I'd also like to celebrate with you as you progress in your journey. Be sure to visit my website, www.graciousleadershipbook.com, and participate in our Gracious Leadership Blog.

I invite you to join in the conversation early on. In so doing, you will learn so much from your colleagues, and they will no doubt learn so much from you.

Additional information is also available on the website regarding the availability of Gracious Leadership speaking engagements and other resources that you may find helpful as you seek to become a good and gracious leader.

Acknowledgements

Within the Epilogue, I shared my heartfelt thanks to my wonderful husband, Richard D'Enbeau, for his unwavering encouragement during the past year. Dick, this book would not have been possible without your loving support. Thank you from the bottom of my heart.

Also to Dick and to my precious daughters, Meredith Meeks Veltri and Mallory Meeks DeLucas, thank you for your loving *patience* as I repeatedly shared with you my exuberance about this work. You know better than anyone that this book has been a labor of love. Thank you for joining me in the excitement about Gracious Leadership and the impact it can have in creating a movement of positive leadership.

I want to acknowledge my dear brother, James Edwin Smith, Jr. (Jim) for joining me in reminiscing about our childhood. Thank you for taking a walk down Memory Lane as we recalled the good times as well as those circumstances that were difficult for children to comprehend. Thank you also for collaborating to assure the accuracy of our childhood stories and in particular, our father's stance on Civil Rights.

Words are inadequate to express my appreciation to Dustin S. Klein, Publisher and Chief Operating Officer of *Smart Business*, who coached me throughout the journey to bring this book to life. Dustin, your insight and wisdom were invaluable as you challenged me to make the manuscript a living tool that current and aspiring leaders can easily use to improve their leadership competencies. Thank you for inspiring me to identify additional stories from my own journey and to provide pragmatic examples of "how" the 13 key ingredients of Gracious Leadership can readily be applied. Simply put, your guidance made *Gracious Leadership: Lead Like You've Never Led Before* a much better book. For the working partnership we have enjoyed in the creation of this work, I sincerely thank you!

Amanda Horvath, Art Director for *Smart Business*, thank you for listening with purpose as you heard my vision for the book's cover and design. You absolutely knocked it out of the park as you portrayed with simplicity and clarity the role of a gracious leader who is taking his or her team to peak performance.

And Abbey Jo Deckard, Editorial Assistant for *Smart Business*, thank you for your attention to detail in assuring that the grammar was proper throughout the book. Please know that my mother and my high school English teachers would be smiling from above right now.

To all the individuals who follow, you are special to me in ways that transcend words. Thank you for teaching me how to lead, for the time you devoted to reviewing the manuscript, for your humbling endorsements, for your insights, support and encouragement, and for the assistance you provided in ways that only you and I know and can appreciate. Thank you also to the individuals whose names I am not publishing to protect the anonymity of their stories. Most importantly, to *all* these individuals, thank you for your friendship: Kerrii Anderson, Kate Finley, John Fleming, Peter Giammalvo, Brett Justice, Joel Lee, Harry R. Jacobson, MD, Debbie Johnson, Linda Kaufmann, Mike Kaufmann, C. Robert Kidder, Cindy Monroe, Aubrey Patterson, Ruby Kathryn Patterson, Amanda Sage, Mike Slubowski, Dwight Smith, Barb Smoot and Dan Wilford.

About the Author

Janet Smith Meeks has devoted nearly four decades of her professional life to healthcare and financial services industries. As a C-suite executive and corporate director, she has vast experience in finance, strategy, operations, marketing, business development and leadership effectiveness.

Janet has served in executive roles for four nationally known healthcare systems, including Trinity Health (the second largest Catholic Healthcare system in the nation) and the prestigious Vanderbilt University Medical Center. Janet spent nine years as president of Mount Carmel St. Ann's Hospital in Westerville, Ohio where she led the organization to peak performance through applying the key ingredients of Gracious Leadership.

As co-founder and CEO of Healthcare Alignment Advisors, Janet uses her experience to guide C-suite executives in creating and implementing strategies to optimize corporate performance within a positive work environment.

Janet is a transformational leader and an innovator who lends her analytical wisdom and business acumen to help organizations become "brilliant at the basics" of business. An award-winning C-suite leader, she has more than two decades of experience commercializing innovative processes and structuring unique models for partnership, joint venture and acquisition to engage stakeholders and align incentives.

By employing the key ingredients of Gracious Leadership throughout her career, along with stressing the importance of the Head-Heart connection, Janet has consistently led highly engaged teams to generate sustained value, profitability, and customer satisfaction through facilitating a culture of compassionate accountability.

A cum laude graduate of the University of Mississippi (UM) in banking and finance, where she played NCAA Division I basketball, Janet also earned her MBA in finance from UM. Janet was inducted into Phi Kappa Phi and she received the Wall Street Journal Award for academic excellence in finance.

Janet enjoys corporate board service as she loves learning about new businesses and industries as well as the challenges they face. In her capacity as a board member, she aspires to ask the right questions with kind candor and grace to help management arrive at the best decisions to optimize organizational performance. Janet has significant breadth and depth of experience within the board room though her many years of service as a corporate director and advisory board member within for-profit and nonprofit sectors.

Additionally, Janet demonstrates a deep commitment to empowering women in business and leadership. She is a member of Women for Economic and Leadership Development (WELD), Women Corporate Directors, National Association of Corporate Directors and Women at the Table (WATT).

Janet reveres her family and treasures the precious time she spends with them. An avid jogger and cycler who enjoys international travel, Janet is a sought-after speaker regarding a broad range of leadership topics. Her quarterly column "Leadership to Inspire Results," is featured in Smart Business magazine.

Notes

Notes